VICTORIAN
BUILDINGS OF
BIRMINGHAM
ROY THORNTON

D1555767

SUTTON PUBLISHING

Birmingham city centre in the early twentieth century.

BUILDING REFERENCE NUMBERS

Note: Figures in brackets note the numbers of buildings covered by the reference.

THE COLMORE ESTATE

1 The College of Art, Margaret Street
2 Birmingham Library, Margaret Street
3(3) 95, 93 and 85–7 Cornwall Street
4 50 & 52 Cornwall Street
5(2) 54 and 56–60 Newhall Street
6 43–51 Newhall Street
7 53 & 55 Church Street
8(2) 41 & 43 and 37 & 39 Church Street
9 158 Edmund Street
10 Skin Hospital, 25 Church Street
11(2) 136 & 138 and 134 Edmund Street
12(3) 133, 125–31 and 121 & 123 Edmund Street
13 Ear & Throat Hospital 105 & 107 Edmund Street
14 17 & 19 Newhall Street and 103 Edmund Street
15 27 & 29 Newhall Street and 106–10 Edmund Street
16 100 & 102 Edmund Street, 44–8 Newhall Street and 78 Cornwall Street
17(2) 98 and 96 Edmund Street

COLMORE ROW & VICTORIA SQUARE

18 Great Western Arcade, Colmore Row to Temple Row
19 Grand Hotel, Colmore Row
20 55 (& 57) Colmore Row, 2–8 Church Street and 38 Barwick Street
21 59 (& 61), 63 & 65 and 67 (& 69) Colmore Row
22(3) 71 & 73, 75 & 77 and 79–83 Colmore Row
23 85–9 Colmore Row
24(2) 37 and 38 Bennett's Hill
25 122 & 124 Colmore Row
26 Council House, Museum & Art Gallery, Victoria Square
27 Chamberlain Memorial, Chamberlain Square
28 Post Office, Victoria Square
29 11 Waterloo Street and 8 Bennett's Hill
30 44 Waterloo Street
31 4 Temple Row West

NEW STREET & THE REST

32(4) 80–3, 84–7, 88–91 and 92 & 93 New Street and 3 & 5 Ethel Street
33 128 New Street
34 35–40 New Street
35 43–5 Cannon Street and 41, 42 & 42A New Street
36 39–42 Cannon Street and 9–15 Needless Alley
37 17 Cannon Street and 10 Cherry Street
38 City Arcade, Union Street to Union Passage

FOREWORD

There were two reasons that led me to undertake this research, the first being that it would be an interest to fill my time when I retired. The second was to expunge any feelings of guilt that might remain about my sentiments towards Victorian architecture at the time I embarked upon the profession of architecture.

In October 1942 I entered an architect's office, that of John B. Surman; at the same time my cousin was working in the office of Cecil E.M. Fillmore. Both of us were enamoured of the International Style, as exemplified in two books by F.R.S. Yorke, *The Modern House* and *The Modern House in England*. I found them stimulating then and still do, but the trouble was that at that time I tended not to look for, or recognise, the qualities of buildings that were significantly different in appearance.

It was a very easy position to adopt, for there had been a general reaction against Victorian design and a desire to get away from 'unnecessary' decorative design features. The black and white photographs in Yorke's books, showing white walls, black openings and flat roofs were, to the young and impressionable mind, a revelation.

The journey through my architectural life has led to a broadening of my appreciation of different styles, although present students might think I have regressed, for I am more likely to praise a scheme by Richard MacCormac, as a fellow admirer of Frank Lloyd-Wright, than one by Zaha Hadid or Daniel Libeskind.

When I started with Mr Surman I was aware that the office had a link with the Victorian period, but this was not significant then and has only become so with the passage of time and now, additionally, with this research.

John B. Surman had taken over the architectural practice of James & Lister Lea, owing, presumably, to the passing of the Architects Registration Acts, and worked on the top floor at 19 Cannon Street, with the remainder of the building occupied by James & Lister Lea. A large proportion of the architectural work of James & Lister Lea comprised the design of public houses, and this work was done by Messrs Brassington and Roberts, as noted in *Birmingham Pubs 1880–1939*, by Alan Crawford and Robert Thorne.

When I joined Mr Surman his only assistant was this Mr Roberts. He had joined James & Lister Lea in 1897, I believe, and the time scale of forty-five years seemed almost unbelievable to me at the time. Now another sixty-three have passed, to provide a link of over one hundred years.

❖   ❖   ❖

The period I decided to study in detail covered roughly the last third of the nineteenth century, a time of great development in Birmingham, carried out under the doctrine of the 'civic gospel', and leading to Birmingham being described as 'the best governed city in the world'. It was not practicable to attempt to study all work that was carried out, so I decided to select certain architects who practised in Birmingham and concentrate on their projects. I chose those who had designed buildings of which I was aware and started to find out about other buildings they had designed. I soon realised that most of these architects did not fit tidily into the last third of the nineteenth century and so, where appropriate, I looked at work carried out earlier, and at the other end went happily into and through the Edwardian period. As I progressed I found that there were several architects who deserved to be included, but by then it was too late. I did not know a lot about the selected architects before I started, and in many cases and ways I don't know much more now. All that I can say with confidence is that I know of many more buildings that they designed than I did at the start. I wanted to find out about the run-of-the-mill buildings they designed and whether they stood out in comparison with their neighbours.

In the case of Newton & Cheatle, as an example, every building of theirs that I knew about was designed or built between 1897 and 1902 and nearly every one still standing is listed. Did they appear from nowhere, design these few buildings and then, after Newton's death, disappear? Looking through the King's Norton Buildings Register the first submission by T.W.F. Newton was in 1885 and the first ones I noted were made in April and September 1887 for two and three houses, respectively, in Park Hill, Moseley. The first application to Birmingham was in April 1888, for a factory and house in Highgate Street, near Porch Street. The first reference to Newton & Cheatle is in 1892, but Newton still made an application to Birmingham in his name only, in January 1893. I have seen few submissions made after Newton's death.

My research did not proceed as easily as I had hoped. It was easy to marry building applications to buildings where these were significant, as in the case of churches and schools, but far more difficult with domestic, commercial and industrial buildings, where the only information, in addition to the description of the building, was the name of the street or road. The earlier applications only gave the name of the applicant, usually the architect, and only in later years was the name of the client added. The plans, at least for those applications made to Birmingham, are kept in the Archives Section of the Birmingham Central Library and all of the assistants there are very helpful, but I discovered, with the majority of the comparatively limited number I tried to see, that one of the following applied: the drawings no longer existed; the drawings existed, but were folded and were too brittle to be opened; I could see the drawings, but they comprised poorly drawn plans, with no site plan or elevations. There were a few that were of interest, including a proposed theatre in Corporation Street by Frank Matcham, but not enough to make the effort worthwhile. Where the owner's name was given, late in the century, I did find, on several occasions, the location of the property in the road from copies of *Kelly's Directory* or the rate-books, but even this was not as successful as I expected. Therefore, in all too many cases, I know that a certain architect designed a certain building in a certain road, but I haven't located it more precisely than that.

As I found more information my research began to branch out in another direction, while not losing sight of my original objective. I obtained details of all the schools erected for the Birmingham School Board, which was not too difficult as nearly all were designed by Martin & Chamberlain. Dr Chris Upton suggested that it might be a suitable subject for inclusion in *Birmingham Historian* and I decided to widen the scope by including all Board schools that were erected within the present city boundary, for there are several other School Boards located within today's boundary. I did this and found that although it might have involved more detailed study, there was a great advantage in looking for specific buildings rather than trying to find everything which might be of interest.

After looking at Board schools I searched for another subject that would be complete in itself and decided to study the original buildings of Corporation Street, between New Street and Steelhouse Lane, for they were all built in a single generation. From there I began to look at specific building types.

At this stage I was doing the research purely for my own interest and enjoyment. I do not remember from where the thought came that it might be turned into a book and whether the idea was mine or stemmed from a suggestion from someone else. However, the idea was there, and I found that Sutton Publishing was prepared to publish my work as a book.

The title I chose for the book, *Victorian Buildings of Birmingham*, meant that I needed to widen the scope of my research and stay within the time limits of the title, although there are three small exceptions where it would have been foolish to stop precisely at 1901, namely: School Boards were set up by the Elementary Education Act of 1870 and abolished by the Education Act of 1902; some of the original buildings of Corporation Street, at the Steelhouse Lane end, were not completed until after 1901, although the last building application was made in 1900; Newton & Cheatle designed a series of exquisite buildings in the city centre between 1897 and 1902 and I thought it would be wrong not to list them all, particularly as one of the later applications was part of a series relating to the City and Midland Arcades leading from New Street. In cases where it was practicable to list all of the buildings of a group, such as Board schools, Corporation Street, hospitals and public buildings, I have mentioned every building of which I am aware, regardless of the quality of the buildings and whether or not they have been demolished, in an attempt to provide as complete a record as possible. In all other cases I have made a selection of buildings that I think are worth seeing, so as to represent the class to which they belong. I have mentioned demolished buildings only when I consider them too important to be ignored. The names of architects are given in all cases where I know them, and I hope this will result in them becoming better known.

The Jewellery Quarter & Surrounds.

BUILDING REFERENCE NUMBERS

Note: Figures in brackets note the numbers of buildings covered by the reference.

1	1–7 Constitution Hill
2	1–4 Hampton Street and 394–6 Summer Lane
3	25 Constitution Hill
4	22A Great Hampton Street and 61 Harford Street
5	44 & 45 Great Hampton Street and 80–96 Hockley Street
6	83 & 84 Great Hampton Street
7	80–82 Great Hampton Street
8	9 Vyse Street
9(2)	27 & 28 and 29 Warstone Lane
10	63 Warstone Lane
11	41–9 Victoria Street
12	12 & 14 Regent Place
13	Victoria Works, Graham Street
14	The Agent Centre, Legge Lane and Frederick Street
15	3, 4 & 5 Legge Lane
16	16 & 17 Newhall Hill
17	New Hall Works, George Street
18	Birmingham Assay Office, Newhall Street

INTRODUCTION

When Queen Victoria came to the throne in 1837 the population of Birmingham was over 110,000 people (1831: 110,914), a significant change from 750 years earlier, when the Domesday survey had indicated a population of ten and a rental value of 20*s* per annum. From being one of the most insignificant places in an area of insignificance, it had become the most important town in an area of ever increasing importance.

The rise of Birmingham began with the granting of two important rights. The first was a grant to Peter de Birmingham in 1166, by King Henry II, to hold a weekly market. It was the only one in the area and established Birmingham as the main local trading area. This was followed, in 1250, by the purchase of the right to hold a four-day fair annually.

Birmingham was comparatively small and much of the land was infertile and, consequently, farming opportunities were limited. Therefore residents were obliged to find other ways to make a living. Many were traders and others became smiths, nail-makers and makers of other items in the metal trade and, by the fourteenth century, Birmingham had become known for its wares.

Development continued through the following centuries and Birmingham became nationally and internationally known for the quality of its swords, guns, small trinkets, snuff boxes, candlesticks, buckles, buttons and almost all things involving iron, brass and other metals. For enterprising young men eager to make their way in the world it was the place to come to, and the fact that it was not chartered was an extra incentive for nonconformists, who were to play such a great part in the development of Birmingham.

The eighteenth century continued to see great changes take place, one being a large increase in the size of manufactories. One of the first was the button-making factory of John Taylor, a name to remember in banking, but the most outstanding was the Soho Manufactory, opened in 1764, by Matthew Boulton, who was joined in partnership, in 1774, by James Watt. Goods of the highest quality were produced at Soho and Boulton was greatly concerned with the establishment of the local assay office. Soho Foundry was opened in 1796, to manufacture the steam engines developed by James Watt. The firm was also a large manufacturer of coins. William Murdoch, the inventor of gas lighting, was an employee of the firm. It was the most important manufactory of its time and, possibly, of all time.

Financial services were needed and John Taylor and Sampson Lloyd joined together to form Taylor's & Lloyd's Bank in 1765, still trading today as Lloyds TSB. In the nineteenth century the Midland Bank was started in the city, so Birmingham had a big impact on the British banking system.

The Lunar Society flourished in the latter years of the eighteenth century. It was based mainly in Birmingham and met frequently at Soho House, Matthew Boulton's home, adjoining his manufactory, but its members came from several towns besides Birmingham. Members met on a night near the full moon for intellectual discussions and to exchange ideas.

It is very important for manufacturers of goods to be able to transport them to their customers, and those in Birmingham, with no navigable river, had to rely on the roads. The roads in the eighteenth century were improved by the introduction of turnpikes, but were never good enough to cope satisfactorily with the volume of traffic that used them. Therefore the advent of the canals was a great boon to the industrialists and many were built to serve Birmingham. However, the heyday of the canals was short. In fifty years railways appeared and Birmingham became, and remains, an important centre in the rail network and has now become equally important in the motorway system.

Queen Victoria came to the throne at a time of great change. Five years before, the Reform Bill had been passed and, by this measure, Birmingham was directly represented in Parliament for the first time, having two members – Thomas Attwood, one of its great heroes, and Joshua Scholefield. The next step in the development of the city was the granting of a Municipal Charter in 1838, which led to a Town Council that had responsibility for an area increased in size to match that of the parliamentary constituency. The reality was not as impressive as it appears, for the Street Commissioners retained control over several matters and that situation was not resolved until the passing of the Birmingham Improvement Act of 1851. Some years later, in 1888, the Council requested that the Queen grant Birmingham the status of a city, and this was done in 1889.

Things did not go smoothly after the granting of the 1838 Charter. Following a Chartist riot, centred on the Bull Ring, in July 1839, the Government more or less suspended the Council for three years. Even afterwards there were problems, for although the majority of councillors were Liberals and initiated many reforms and developments, there was a group on the Council, known as the 'economists', who succeeded in blocking or slowing down many proposals.

Then came a dramatic change, led by a group of civic-minded citizens, mainly non-conformists, and including two of the most influential men in the history of Birmingham. Both had been born in London and yet, together with many others, in not much more than a generation, they transformed Birmingham from a poorly run town to 'the best governed city in the world'. George Dawson was the Minister of the Church of the Saviour, which he had founded, in Edward Street. Dawson preached the

George Dawson.

doctrine of the 'civic gospel', stating that one's religious beliefs could not be separated from one's public duty. It is hard today to appreciate the effect of his oratory, but it would have been to no purpose if there had been no one prepared to put his words into action. But there were several people, and notable among them, although not the first, was Joseph Chamberlain, a colossus in local and national politics in the late nineteenth century and a passionate believer in education. In local politics he is remembered best for his achievements during his three years as mayor from 1873 to 1876, when the water and gas supplies were taken under Council control and the Improvement Scheme was passed, leading to the construction of Corporation Street. The change had started before that and from the 1860s onwards there was a huge surge in building activity, both public and private, and it is with the best of that with which I am most concerned.

❖ ❖ ❖

The Victorian period saw the architectural 'Battle of the Styles' between Classical and Gothic, brought about by the Gothic revival. At the commencement of Queen Victoria's reign the Classical style predominated, exemplified in Birmingham by buildings such as the Town Hall, Market Hall, Curzon Street station and the Midland Bank, on the corner of Bennett's Hill and Waterloo Street, all just built or in the process of being built. The Gothic revival had received a tremendous boost with the condition imposed on the competitors for the design of the new Houses of Parliament that the only acceptable styles for the building were Gothic and Elizabethan, both looked on as British. The competition was

Joseph Chamberlain.

won by Charles Barry, assisted by A.W.N. Pugin, a happy choice for Birmingham, as only two years before he had won the competition to design King Edward VI School in New Street and was now involved in its building, assisted by Pugin. Barry was not, by conviction, a Gothic architect, but he hardly needed to be while he had Pugin at his side, for Pugin was the most passionate advocate of Gothic architecture in the country. Architects practising outside Birmingham were given few opportunities to design buildings in the town, but Pugin was lucky, for he was responsible for four, which are listed in the chapter on religious buildings.

Two instances of the contrast between the Classical and Gothic styles have always fascinated me. I have had to settle for illustrations, for only one of the buildings still survives. The first contrasts the Exchange Building in Stephenson Place, opened in 1865 and demolished a century later, with the Midland Bank, erected on the corner of New Street and Stephenson Place, in 1867–9. This building still stands and is occupied today by Waterstone's, the bookseller, and is Grade II listed. The buildings could not be more different and yet were designed by the same architect, Edward Holmes, within a short time of each other.

The other instance has different architects, but the same client. The architect of the Classical building for the Birmingham and Midland Institute was E.M. Barry. The building was on the corner of Radcliffe Place and Paradise Street and was erected in 1855–7. An extension was built in 1881, in Paradise Street, the architect being John Henry Chamberlain of the firm Martin & Chamberlain, honorary secretary of the

Exchange Building, Stephenson Place (demolished).

128 New Street (Waterstone's).

Birmingham and Midland Institute, Radcliffe Place with its extension beyond (demolished).
(Birmingham Central Library)

Institute from 1865. Of all architects in Birmingham, Chamberlain was possibly the one with the strongest and most fixed architectural convictions, and Barry's building did not conform with his beliefs. Consequently, it would be difficult to find two buildings standing next to each other that had so little in common as the Institute and its extension. Ironically, on the other side of the Institute, in Radcliffe Place, stood the Birmingham Central Lending and Reference Library, matching, owing to the conditions imposed, the Institute building. The architect for the library when it was built in 1865 was William Martin, and for the rebuilding after the fire of 1879, Martin & Chamberlain.

As the century progressed there was a much greater use of decoration and ornament and the Classical style gave way to the Renaissance, to allow for increased freedom of expression. The principal facing materials had been, and continued to be, brick and stone, but, in the later years another material, terracotta, became popular, particularly after the construction of the Victoria Law Courts. By the end of the century there was a turn towards a simpler form of building, springing in the first place from domestic architecture, using such terms as the Vernacular and Queen Anne revival and coming, primarily, from the Arts and Crafts movement.

The Victorian period saw buildings of many architectural styles, and varieties within those styles, so that it is hard to categorise many Victorian buildings, and yet it is not hard to recognise one as Victorian. In the twentieth century there followed a period of revulsion towards Victorian architecture and design in general, and its many virtues were ignored. That time has passed and now there is a greater appreciation of the Victorian period than for a hundred years. Birmingham, on the whole, used its own architects and there are not many examples of work by nationally known architects. However, they do exist and with them are many buildings by local architects of no small ability, and I hope you will be encouraged to look for them and at them.

ACKNOWLEDGEMENTS

I am grateful to the members of staff of the Archives and the Local Studies Sections of Birmingham Central Library for the helpful and courteous way in which they dealt with all my requests for information. I should give a special mention to Patrick Baird, who I know outside the library, and therefore, occasionally, burdened him to a greater extent, which he accepted uncomplainingly.

I do not know what it is like to deal with would-be authors, but it cannot be easy, particularly when they are growing old and with fading faculties, but Simon Fletcher of Sutton Publishing has treated me with great patience and given much welcome encouragement. In addition, when it was realised that the number of library photographs we could use would have to be reduced, he took many photographs to help the book and me and I appreciate this greatly.

CHAPTER 1

MARTIN & CHAMBERLAIN

INTRODUCTION

T he architectural practice of Martin & Chamberlain was probably the most important in Birmingham during the last third of the nineteenth century, almost exactly the period in which the firm practised under that name. It may not be completely accurate, but it is reasonable to say that it developed from the practice of Daniel R. Hill, for whom William Martin worked as chief assistant and later as partner.

Hill had wanted to be the Borough Architect and the idea was discussed, but nothing happened, although he did design several public buildings. When Hill died, in 1857, the Council passed a unanimous tribute to his memory and to his many public services. The public buildings with which he was concerned were Winson Green Prison, 1844–9; Mental Asylum, Lodge Road, 1849, now All Saints' Hospital, Grade II listed; Kent Street Public Baths, the first in Birmingham, now demolished; work on the public offices, 11 and 12 Moor Street, with additions, now demolished.

Other buildings he designed included St James's Church, Mere Green Road, Sutton Coldfield, in 1834/5, Grade II listed; St Luke's Church of England Primary School, St Luke's Road, now demolished; Protestant Dissenting Charity School, Graham Street/Newhall Hill, 1839; St John's Church, Walmley Road, Sutton Coldfield, 1845, Grade II listed; All Saints' National School, All Saints' Street/Lodge Road, 1848, now demolished; Asylum for Licensees, Bristol Road, 1849.

William Martin was born in Somerset in 1829 and came to Birmingham, where he was articled to T. Plevins. He had been responsible for the following buildings (presumably among others) before going into partnership with Chamberlain in 1864: extension to the General Hospital, Summer Lane, 1857; addition of four three-storey blocks to the Mental Asylum in Lodge Road, 1861; Public Baths, Northwood Street, 1862, now demolished; Central Library, 1864, destroyed by fire, January 1879; St David's Church, Bissell Street. Martin died in 1899 and his sons changed the name of the practice to Martin & Martin and it continues today, with the name of Martin in the title.

John Henry Chamberlain was born in Leicester in 1831, the son of a Calvinist Baptist minister. He was a pupil of H. Goddard of Leicester and strongly influenced by John Ruskin. He came to Birmingham in 1856 to design a shop for his uncle and carried out other work, including the buildings listed below, before joining William Martin in partnership at a time when he was considering emigrating to New Zealand. The shop at 28 and 29 Union Street built for his uncle, now demolished; house,

John Henry Chamberlain.

12 Ampton Road, Edgbaston, 1858, Grade II listed; All Saints' School, Hearn Street, 1863, now demolished; Methodist church, St Martin's Street, Islington, 1864, now demolished.

Chamberlain was Professor of Architecture at Queen's College and, from 1865, honorary secretary of the Birmingham and Midland Institute. He was a good public speaker and lecturer, and prominent in the civic and cultural life of Birmingham, becoming a magistrate shortly before his death, which occurred in October 1883, one hour after he had concluded a lecture on Exotic Art at the Birmingham and Midland Institute.

Chamberlain was recognised as the outstanding architect practising in Birmingham during his lifetime, and if a poll was conducted to decide who was the best architect ever to practise in Birmingham it is likely that he would head the list. He was a man of strong architectural convictions, and if a client wanted a building designed in the Renaissance style it is unlikely he would have approached Chamberlain. Rather naturally, he was the dominant design partner in the practice and there were very few buildings that were not designed by him, although there are a few that do not bear his stamp.

The position of William Martin is not so easy to evaluate. I have seen mention of his technical and planning abilities, both very important, but I believe the high standard maintained by the practice after the death of Chamberlain must owe a lot to William Martin. After Chamberlain died, Martin took his own sons, Frederick and Herbert, into the partnership. Frederick is normally given the credit for two outstanding buildings, Spring Hill Library and 17 to 19 Newhall Street, both unlike any other buildings ever designed by the practice. Now it probably matters little where the credit lies.

I do not know whether Martin & Chamberlain ever had the wish to be the Borough Architect, but, if so, it was more or less achieved in effect, if not in title, for the practice was responsible for a substantial proportion of the public buildings designed in the last third of the century. Some of the most important projects I shall list, separating the public commissions from the rest, but I will not attempt to describe them, as there was a consistent design ethic, with the one or two exceptions referred to above. However, several will receive brief descriptions in various chapters where they are mentioned.

PUBLIC BUILDINGS

Schools

At the first meeting of the Birmingham School Board in November 1870 the practice was appointed Architect to the Board. It was an appointment that lasted until January 1902, by which time the original partners were dead and the name of the practice had been changed to Martin & Martin. The Education Act of 1902 abolished School Boards and passed responsibility to local authorities. During its existence the Birmingham School Board built fifty-one new schools, of which all but four were designed by Martin & Chamberlain (the last three in the name of Martin & Martin). In addition, existing buildings were modified for temporary or permanent use and most of the new buildings were altered and extended. Martin & Chamberlain also designed the School Board offices in Edmund Street. It must have been the most rewarding appointment ever awarded to an architect in Birmingham. A list of the buildings is provided in the chapter on Board Schools.

Other educational projects included the College of Art, Margaret Street, 1881–5, with an extension in Cornwall Street, 1893, Grade I listed; school and house, Rubery, for King's Norton School Board, 1883; Branch School of Art, Vittoria Street: additions to and adaptation of existing building, 1890, followed by additions in 1900, Grade II listed.

Hospitals

D.R. Hill and William Martin designed hospital buildings, and these commissions formed a significant body of work in the practice. Although in many cases it may not be correct to include the project as a public building, as all the projects served the public it is reasonable to include them here: workhouse, Western Road: extension in 1865, now demolished; Children's Hospital, Steelhouse Lane: Out-Patients' Department, 1869, alterations and additions in 1899, now demolished; Women's Hospital: Out-Patients' Department, Upper Priory, 1871, now demolished; Queen's Hospital, Bath Row: west block, built in 1873, Grade II listed; Mental Asylum, Lodge Road: fifty-bed dormitory built in 1878, alterations and additions in 1888, Grade II listed; Asylum, Rubery Hill, Northfield: built in 1882, at a cost of £132,000, extensions added in 1890 and 1893, demolished, except for Lodge, Chapel and Superintendent's House, all Grade II listed; Fever Hospital, Lodge Road: two wards and administration offices built in 1884, administration accommodation and pavilions added in 1895, Grade II listed; Children's Hospital, Broad Street: alterations in 1899.

Libraries

Central Library, Radcliffe Place: rebuilt in 1880 after the fire in 1879, now demolished; Constitution Hill: built in 1881, now demolished; Spring Hill: built in 1891 and Grade II* listed.

Public Baths

Northwood Street: built in 1862 with extensions carried out in 1874 and 1876, now demolished; Monument Road: built in 1883, now demolished.

Police and Fire Stations

Police Station, 112 Moseley Street: built in 1877, no longer used as a police station, Grade II listed; Police Station, Dudley Road/Summerfield Road: built in 1878, now demolished; Police Station, 248–52 Coventry Road, built in 1879, now demolished; Central Fire Station, Upper Priory: built in 1883, now demolished.

College of Art, Margaret Street.

Library, Spring Hill.

Waterworks

Pumping Station, Waterworks Road, Ladywood: built in 1870, Grade II listed; Pumping Station, Bristol Road South, Longbridge: built in 1870; Pumping Station, Bristol Road, Selly Oak: and two cottages built in 1879; Pumping Station, Aston: built in 1881, comprising engine, boiler house and stack; water tower, Victoria Park, Small Heath: built in 1888; hydraulic supply stores, Dalton Street: built in 1890, for Birmingham Waterworks.

Housing

Twenty-two artisans' dwellings, Ryder Street, built in 1889, the first council houses in Birmingham, now demolished.

Another important appointment for the firm was as Surveyor for the Improvement Scheme resulting in the construction of Corporation Street.

OTHER PROJECTS

City Centre

19–23 Corporation Street: for Marris & Norton, 1880, destroyed by fire in 1888; 80–6 Corporation Street: for Avery's, 1880, now demolished; 150–8 Corporation Street: for Birmingham Household Supply Association, 1880, now demolished; Joseph Chamberlain Memorial, Chamberlain Square: 1880, Grade II listed; Birmingham and Midland Institute, Paradise Street: extension, 1881, now demolished; 114 and 116 Corporation Street: for Ray & Prosser, 1883, now demolished; 32 Bull Street: alterations and additions, now demolished; Grand Hotel, Barwick Street: extensions in 1889 and 1893; 17 and 19 Newhall Street and 103 Edmund Street, 1896, Grade I listed; 99 and 100 Bull Street: rebuilding in 1896, now demolished.

Churches

I am confident only about two, namely St Stephen's, Serpentine Road, Selly Oak, 1870–1, Grade II listed; St John the Evangelist's, Stratford Road, Sparkhill, Grade II listed. I have seen two others mentioned: St Nicholas's, Lower Tower Street, which has been demolished, and South Street Methodist Church, Harborne, but am not sure that they were designed by Martin & Chamberlain.

Pumping Station, Waterworks Road, Edgbaston.

17 and 19 Newhall Street.

Educational Buildings
New School, Severn Street: 1879; King Edward VI Grammar School for Boys, Camp Hill: 1883, Grade II listed; schools, Newton Street: for St Philip's, built in 1883, now demolished; Girls' High School, Hagley Road: built in 1884; King Edward VI Grammar School for Girls, Camp Hill: 1896, Grade II listed.

Houses
All of the houses are in Edgbaston, unless otherwise indicated: 50 Carpenter Road: built in 1870(?); Berrow Court, Berrow Drive: built 1870–5, Grade II* listed, the home of the parents of Harriet Kenrick, Joseph Chamberlain's first wife, and in recent years a hotel; Hampden Villa, 19 Greenfield Crescent built in 1875; four houses, Edgbaston Lane (now Edgbaston Road): built in 1875; The Grove, Harborne: extensions in 1875, an interior is in the Victoria and Albert Museum; Whetstone, Farquhar Road/Somerset Road: built in 1878, but now demolished – the home of J.H. Chamberlain and rather forbidding; Highbury, Yew Tree Road, Moseley built in 1879, Grade II* listed – the home of Joseph Chamberlain, now owned by the city; Harborne Hall: extensions and alterations in 1884; twelve cottages at Stirchley for Cadbury Brothers: built in 1885; six houses, Langley Road, Small Heath: built in 1887; 24 Priory Road: built in 1893, Grade II listed – built for J.T. Bunce, editor of the *Birmingham Post*, and now part of Priory Hospital.

St John the Evangelist's, Stratford Road.

Industrial and Commercial

This type of project never formed a large part of the work of the practice, except for the commercial work in the city centre. The work I have researched covers a ten-year period: warehouse, Ernest Street: 1882; warehouse, Lower Priory: 1883; Elliot Metal Co., Selly Oak: offices built in 1885; 266 and 266X Broad Street and 2 Gas Street: shop, offices and warehouse for Joseph Sturge, built in 1887 with extensions in 1896, Grade II listed; Southall, Dalton Street: factory and warehouse built in 1888, now demolished; Ingall, Parsons & Clive, 206–20 Bradford Street: alterations and additions to factory; Lionel Street Hinge Co., Holt Street: offices built in 1892; Isaac Hollis & Son, Lench Street: warehouse and shopping, 1892.

SUMMARY

It is sad, if not surprising, that so many of these buildings have been demolished, but there are many left to appreciate and to realise what a high standard was achieved and maintained. It may not always be possible to say with certainty that a building is by Martin & Chamberlain, as exemplified by the church of St Cyprian at Hay Mills, and one would not have recognised the Central Library and Queen's Hospital as Martin & Chamberlain buildings, but these are the odd exceptions in the work of a practice that maintained a consistent style, which makes it comparatively easy to believe that the building you are looking at was designed by Martin & Chamberlain. It was a lucky day for the architectural scene in Birmingham when the two principals entered into partnership.

CHAPTER 2

PUBLIC BUILDINGS

COUNCIL OFFICES

The great increase in the population of Birmingham has been achieved, to a great extent, by the takeover of neighbouring authorities. These authorities, which provided facilities such as libraries, public baths and police stations, needed accommodation to carry out the necessary administration. I have not made a great study of these facilities, but I am aware of the ones listed below:

Town Hall, Mill Street, Sutton Coldfield. Most of the residents of Sutton Coldfield will know these premises as the Masonic Buildings and this is not unreasonable, for they ceased to be the Town Hall in 1906, when its functions were transferred to the building opened in 1865 as the Royal Hotel after the extension of the railway to Sutton Coldfield. This building, facing King Edward's Square, acted as the Council House until the takeover of Sutton Coldfield by Birmingham in 1974, and is in use today as the Neighbourhood Office.

However, it is the building in Mill Street designed by George Bidlake and opened in 1859 that is of interest to me. From the Parade, Mill Street rises steeply until it joins High Street and, although the building is near the lower end of Mill Street, it still occupies a very prominent position when viewed from the Parade, which is to the south.

Town Hall, Mill Street, Sutton Coldfield.

The main feature is a projecting tower, originally in four stages, with clocks in the gables of the roof structure. Unfortunately, the top two stages have been demolished so that the tower is roofed from the top of the second level, in line with the eaves level of the main two-storey building. The dominant facing material is red facing brick, well supported by stone, blue brick and ceramic tile banding, which runs beneath the bracketed eaves cornice, the string courses at the springing level of the arches to the windows and the first-floor entablature. In general the windows are lancet designed, and to Mill Street they are in single, double and triple arrangements. There is a projecting triple window feature on the south elevation, to the left of the tower, and the south-west corner is splayed at ground-floor level, with a single window inserted. The entrance to the building is in the west face of the tower, up steps leading from Mill Street, and there is a coat of arms above the entrance doors. A plinth from the ground-floor window-sill level projects out in three steps down to ground level.

Council House, Victoria Square. The commission for this building was awarded to Yeoville Thomason after he won the competition for the design of the building, and it was erected between 1874 and 1879. Many of the departments were transferred to Baskerville House in Broad Street when it was built, just before the Second World War, but this building is now being refurbished to be put to new use and Council departments are now spread over several buildings. A description of the Council House is given in the chapter on Colmore Row and Victoria Square.

Council Offices and Library, Soho Road, Handsworth. This building was erected in 1878–9 for Handsworth UDC and was designed by Alexander & Henman. The building is still used as a library and is described under that heading, and also as a college of further education.

Council Offices and Library, Albert Road and Witton Road, Aston was built for Aston Manor Council in 1882 and was designed by William Henman. Once again, as the building still functions as a library it is described under that heading.

Council Offices, Stratford Road, Sparkhill. These offices were designed in 1900 by Arthur Harrison, for Yardley (Rural) District Council. The building is two storeys high, seven bays wide and built in brick and stone. The central bay has a two-storey bow window and in the outside bays there are canted bay windows at ground-floor level. Polygonal buttresses rise from these bay windows, culminating in pinnacles at the sides and the apexes of the gables over. The entrances are in the second and sixth bays. On the right side of the building there is a square clock tower with pinnacles and lantern cupola.

LIBRARIES

Before public libraries were provided there were private and subscription libraries, of which there were several in Birmingham. The most important one, which subsequently became the Birmingham Library, was established in 1779. From 1797 until 1899 this library was in its own premises in Union Street, designed by William Hollins. It then moved to a new building, designed by Cossins & Peacock, on the corner of Margaret Street and Cornwall Street, now owned by the Birmingham and Midland Institute, and Grade II listed.

In 1850 the Free Libraries Act was passed, but approval was not given in Birmingham until 21 February 1860. Following this, at a meeting on 15 May, the Free Libraries Committee 'recommended the establishment of a Central Reference Library, Lending Library, Newsroom and Art Gallery, near the Town Hall, and of three branch libraries; one for the northern district, near St George's Church; another near Gosta Green, for the eastern district; and a third in the vicinity of Bradford Street, for the southern district'. These recommendations were approved by the Council.

The first of these libraries, the Northern, in Constitution Hill, was opened in an existing building in April 1861. When the lease expired in 1881 it was replaced by a new building, also in Constitution Hill, designed by Martin & Chamberlain, which was demolished after the Second World War. An additional library, the Adderley Park Library (which I have seen ascribed to G.E. Street), was presented to the town by C.R. Adderley and opened in 1864. In September 1865 the Central (and Western) Lending Library opened in Radcliffe Place, followed, in the same building, by the Central Reference Library, opened on 26 October 1866. This building was designed by William Martin, although originally E.M. Barry, the architect of the adjoining Birmingham and Midland Institute, had been appointed. However, his proposals were too expensive and the commission was then awarded to Martin. After the fire of 1879 the replacement building of 1882 was also designed by Martin & Chamberlain. This later building was demolished to make way for the present one, built in 1973. On the same day in October 1866 as the Central Reference Library was opened, the Southern District Library was also opened in Heath Mill Lane, Deritend. This building was designed by Bateman & Corser, as was the Gosta Green (Eastern) Library. The foundation stone of the Eastern Library was laid on this same busy October day and the building, on the corner of Legge Street and Aston Road, opened to the public in 1868. The only one of these libraries remaining is the one in Heath Mill Lane, a two-gabled Gothic building of brick with stone dressings, which has recently been refurbished, after years of neglect, by the owner of the Custard Factory. Birmingham now rested on its laurels until the 1890s.

Council Offices and Library, Soho Road, Handsworth. *(Birmingham Central Library)*

Handsworth UDC Council Offices and the Library in Soho Road were designed by Alexander & Henman in 1878–9. This is an attractively composed, asymmetrical, mainly two-storey building, Grade II listed, built in red brick with stone dressings. The entrance to the Council offices was through a rather heavy clock tower, with a squat spire and gables and the library entrance was on the left side facing the road, through a projecting polygonal bay with an octagonal lantern over it.

Perry Barr Institute, a simple Gothic building, was built in 1874, on Birchfield Road, and became a library in 1886. Both buildings were taken over by Birmingham in 1911 and still function as libraries.

Aston Manor Council Offices and Library, on the corner of Albert Road and Witton Road, was opened on 5 January 1882. The architect was William Henman. It is a two-storey plus attic building of red brick with stone dressings. There is a polygonal corner tower with five bays, each three windows wide, along each street face. The second and fourth bays project and have gables. At the extension of the city boundary in 1911 the building came under the control of Birmingham and it is still used as a library.

After a gap of over twenty years several attractive libraries were built in the 1890s and they are still standing today and worth seeing:

Saltley Road, Nechells, now known as Bloomsbury Library, Nechells Parkway, was built in 1891–2. It was designed by Cossins & Peacock and is Grade II listed. The building is faced with red brick and terracotta and was built on a corner site, with the entrance on the corner with a clock tower above.

High Street, Harborne, is an exception in that it was built in 1870 as a Masonic hall, and converted to a library in 1892.

Spring Hill, designed by Martin & Chamberlain, is a gem and deservedly Grade II* listed. It is one of two buildings attributed to Frederick Martin during the days when the practice was known as Martin & Chamberlain. Both are outstanding, and different from any other buildings produced by the firm. The building is Gothic in red brick and terracotta, with many gables, and the entrance is on the corner in an elegant tower surmounted by a spire. The library was in grave danger of being demolished when the ring road was proposed, but there was such an outcry that the road was diverted, thus saving the library.

Green Lane, Small Heath, designed by Henry Martin (not connected with Martin & Chamberlain), and Grade II listed, was built in 1893 and is another building faced with red brick and terracotta. It is on a corner site of triangular shape. The entrance at the junction of the two roads is set in a circular clock tower and separated from the main library hall by a top-lit vestibule. In 1902 a public baths building, also designed by Henry Martin, was erected on the widest part of the site. The building has not been used as a library for some years, but it is still used for other purposes.

Left: Library, Green Lane, Small Heath.

Below: Balsal Heath Library.

Stratford Road, Sparkhill, was built in 1894, to the designs of Arthur Harrison, and is the only one of these new libraries not to be listed, but this should not stop you from visiting it. The facing materials are of the usual red brick and terracotta and it has the obligatory clock tower, capped with a cupola.

Moseley Road, Balsall Heath, designed by Cossins & Peacock and Grade II* listed, is the last of the buildings of this phase, erected in 1895–6, and to mark this, although the bricks are red, the terracotta is buff in colour. The entrance to the building is on the right side, in the clock tower, with the library hall to the left, lit by three large windows built off a terracotta plinth and capped with three terracotta pediments. To the left of the library is the building of 1907 that houses the public baths, which is urgently in need of funds for restoration work.

PUBLIC BATHS

Following an enabling Act of Parliament in 1846, the Council instructed Daniel R. Hill to design public baths on a site in Kent Street and these were opened in 1851, providing sixty-nine private baths, two swimming baths and three plunge baths. There was also a washing department, with twenty-five washing stalls and thirty-two drying horses. However, the stalls were little used, so they were converted into Turkish baths in 1878. Pevsner described the building as 'a thin brick Gothic', but from the rather obscure photograph I have seen, taken at an oblique angle, I find it hard to reconcile the description, especially as the building no longer exists.

Woodcock Street, Aston, was the next baths to open, in 1860, and the architect was Edward Holmes. This building is now the University of Aston Sports Centre and is Grade II listed. A large extension, built in 1926, providing a first-class swimming bath and a gala bath screens the original exterior, but the original interior remains.

Northwood Street baths, designed by William Martin, were opened in 1862 on the corner of Livery Street, with extensions built in 1874 and 1878 by Martin & Chamberlain. I know nothing about this building, other than it no longer exists, but the fact that it had two extensions in a short period of time suggests there was a time when it was a well-used facility.

Monument Road, Ladywood, was the last baths built by Birmingham in the Victorian era, in 1883, the architect being Martin & Chamberlain. Neither this building nor its successor survives.

The only other Victorian public baths to be constructed within the present city boundaries, so far as I know, were those built in Victoria Road, Aston, in 1892. I used to go there for swimming lessons from school. It was built in red brick and terracotta and, from a photograph taken at an angle, it had an oriel window over the central entrance, with a gable above and triangular pediments to each side, at the sill level of the oriel, above a circular panel. There were also triangular pediments over the arcading to the two side entrances. The building was demolished some time ago.

PUBLIC MARKETS

The market area in Birmingham was centred mainly on the Bull Ring and the area to the south of it. This still applies, but all of the Victorian buildings have disappeared, mainly to make way for the redevelopment of the 1960s.

The Market Hall in the Bull Ring, although I have seen a *Kelly's Directory* giving the address as High Street, does not properly qualify to be in this book, as it was built in 1833–5, before Victoria came to the throne, but, as it was one of the best-known and loved buildings in Birmingham, I have considered it worthy of inclusion. It was built in stone in the Classical style, designed by Charles Edge, and stood on the corner of Bell Street. The building was left as a shell after a bombing raid in August 1940, but was used as an open-air market until it was demolished in the 1960s.

The Wholesale Fish Market was built in the Bull Ring, on the corner of Bell Street and opposite the Market Hall, in 1869. It was a stone building, with twin pediments over an arcade of six tall, semicircular-headed windows to the Bull Ring frontage. The architect was J.J. Bateman and a large extension was added in 1884, to the design of W. Spooner Till, the Borough Surveyor.

Smithfield Market, as it came to be called, was opened in 1817, after the Street Commissioners acquired the site of the old Birmingham Manor House early in the nineteenth century and filled in the moat. It was used for the sale of cattle, horses, pigs and sheep, together with hay and straw. In 1883–4 W. Spooner Till designed the

Wholesale Vegetable Market on part of the site and, at the same time, F.B. Osborn & Reading designed St Martin's Hotel and shops. Additions to the Market were designed by F.B. Osborn & Reading in 1892 and 1900–3. The Market was a large, imposing, brick building.

The Meat Market in Bradford Street, stretching through to Cheapside at the rear and Sherlock Street at the side, was designed in 1894–5 by Essex, Nicol & Goodman. There was a tall central building, with two entrances from Bradford Street, each with an arcade of five semicircular-headed windows. At each side, there were semicircular-headed entrances, separating the main building from lower side buildings. The facing materials were red brick and yellow terracotta. There was a circular building on the corner of Bradford Street and Sherlock Street, which, I assume, had some connection with the market.

Pig Market, in Montague Street, Bordesley designed by Cossins, Peacock & Bewlay in 1900, was the last building to be erected, and away from the main market area. Unfortunately, the pig dealers would not use it for various reasons, including legal disputes. Later it was designated as a market for pigs, sheep and cattle and later still came to be referred to as a cattle market.

POLICE AND FIRE STATIONS

When I made a start on police and fire stations I did not expect to find many problems. For, very quickly, I found the locations of all the police stations in Birmingham in 1900 and the locations, but not the addresses, of the stations that came into Birmingham in 1911. These were not too difficult to find in most cases, although in some instances there seemed to be more than one station. The difficulties arose when I tried to discover information about the buildings, which was my main and almost only object. I realised that it was unlikely that most of the buildings would be of interest, architecturally, but expected to unearth some, particularly as three of the stations were designed by Martin & Chamberlain. However, none of the drawings of these three survived. I have not found any photographs of the buildings and two of them have been demolished; the third still exists, but not as a police station.

The situation is worse for fire stations, as most that I was aware of were built in the early years of the twentieth century. Many of the early ones were built as part of, or adjacent to, a police station and in such cases I shall make mention of them.

Policing in Birmingham in 1900 was divided into five divisions, lettered from 'A' to 'E', and I shall start by naming the stations responsible for the five divisions, in that order.

Newton Street station, designed by Sir Aston Webb and Ingress Bell, was built as part of an extension to the Victoria Law Courts in 1892–3 and is part of the Grade I listed complex. Even being part of such an important building does not guarantee that it will be suitable, and after the First World War it was deemed to be unsatisfactory for its purpose, so a new station was built in 1932, at 52–60 Steelhouse Lane.

Ladywood Road police station and the adjacent fire station were sited next to the Lench's Trust almshouses, which still stand at 231 Ladywood Middleway. The station was two storeys high and three bays wide, the outer bays having two windows at each level and the narrower centre bay having one window at first-floor level. The centre bay was slightly advanced and capped by a triangular pediment. The entrance was in this bay and the round-headed opening had a grotesque arrangement of quoins as a surround. The main facing material was brick, with stone features and dressings. An extension, designed by Cresswell & Harrison, was added in 1879. After a new police station was built in 1965 it was no longer needed, and so it was demolished.

Kenyon Street station was on the south side, towards Caroline Street, with a fire station next door. It closed in 1972 when a new station opened in Warstone Lane. The building was three storeys high, with what appears to be a bracketed cornice and varied unattractive details to the windows.

Duke Street station was established in 1847 and was close to the public baths in Woodcock Street. However, both Duke Street and the police station graciously gave way to Aston University.

112 Moseley Street was designed in 1877 as the first of three police stations by Martin & Chamberlain and is the only one to survive. It ceased to be a divisional headquarters in 1942, when the baton was passed to Acocks Green, but continued as a police station until 1959, when a new one was built in Bradford Street, with its front entrance in Moseley Street. The Grade II listed building is three storeys high, plus an attic, and is built in red brick and terracotta. There are three large gables decorated with cut brickwork and terracotta and the coupled and single windows at first-floor levels have arches with blind tympana set in terracotta panels and decorative roundels. A large segmental arched entrance leads to the courtyard. The first Birmingham home of John Henry Newman was on this site.

On a more humble level, there were outstations at the following addresses:

Dudley Road, Summerfield Park. This was the second station designed by Martin & Chamberlain, in 1878, but

Old Police Station, 112 Moseley Street.

was demolished some years ago, although there is a police station on the site, or close to it. There was also a fire station.

410 Nechells Park Road. This station was replaced by one in Bloomsbury Street, Nechells, built in 1905.

248–52 Coventry Road. I assume that this station, between Greenway Street and Green Lane, Small Heath, is the one designed by Martin & Chamberlain in 1879. It was closed in 1976 after a new station was built at Stechford, and demolished in the 1980s.

Prince Arthur Road station, Saltley. You will look in vain for this road, for, in a democratic gesture, it relinquished its title and became plain George Arthur Road. The station was the last building on the west side before St Saviour's Road and included a fire station. The building was two storeys high, with a cornice and balustrade, and three bays wide. The centre bay was narrower and recessed and incorporated the entrance, which had a segmented head. It was built of brick and had stone quoins and dressings. The station came to Birmingham in 1891, when the city boundary was extended, at a cost of £2,800. Unfortunately, this turned out to be rather an extravagant waste of public money, for there is no longer a police station in George Arthur Road.

Edwardes Street station, Balsall Heath. In a typical case of keeping up (or in Prince Arthur Road's case, keeping down would be more appropriate) with the Jones's, Edwardes Street changed its name to Edward Road. This was another station, at no. 48, which was absorbed by Birmingham in 1891, at a cost of £5,250. However, it may have been better value, for there is still a police station in Edward Road, close to Moseley Road, but, if my information is correct, it has moved to the opposite side of the road.

204 and 206 Bridge Street West. Most of the street has disappeared in the massive redevelopment of the area. The section housing the police station, close to Summer Lane, remains, but not the police station, which was replaced by a new one, built in the late 1920s.

90 Wellington Road, Edgbaston. I know nothing about this police station, other than it was the last building but one on the south side of the road, before Sir Harry's Road, and it is not there today, at least not as a police station. I should imagine it was a rather superior sort of place, with a good class of prisoner.

High Street station, Harborne, designed by G. Kenwick in 1896, was on the corner of Greenfield Road. It was a two-storey building of no great architectural distinction and no longer exists.

Other police stations were taken over on the extension of the city boundary in 1911. These were Stirchley (Victoria Road); Sparkhill (Stratford Road); Acocks Green (Warwick Road, near to Westley Road); Hay Mills; Aston Petty Session House and

Aston (Victoria Road, including Police Court); Erdington (Wilton Road); and Handsworth (Thornhill Road, including Court House). The only one that I believe is still operating from its original building is Stratford Road and the only building that I would like to comment on is **Hay Mills**, even though I do not know its location.

The reason for choosing it is that I have seen a photograph of the building, taken in 1910. There was a central station, flanked on each side by two houses. The station building is two storeys high, with an attic, and is three bays wide. The entrance is in the centre bay, with a two-light window over it. There are buttresses from first-floor level, terminating in pinnacles, flanking the gables of the outer bays. The facing materials are brick and stone. Each house has a canted bay window at ground-floor level. The building changed its function at some stage and became the Old Bill and Bull public house. I do not know whether it is still in use as a pub, as it is not listed in the telephone directory.

One building that never came under the control of Birmingham was the **Sutton Coldfield Police Court**, **Station Street**. It was in use from the 1880s until 1960, when it was replaced by a new police station and magistrates' court, with a new fire station next to it, all of these coming under the control of Birmingham in 1974. The old station was pulled down in 1967. The title 'Police Court', shown in a panel on the building, indicated that the function of the building was more than that of a mere police station. It was a two-storey building, with attics, faced in brick and stone and reasonably supplied with gables with hipped cappings.

I have mentioned several fire stations attached to police stations. There were also fire stations in Chester Street, Aston, Soho Road, Handsworth and Stratford Road/Court Road, Sparkhill, this last one to a design of A. Harrison in 1900, but there must have been others. However, the most important fire station in Victorian Birmingham was the **Central fire station in Upper Priory**, which was designed by Martin & Chamberlain and erected in 1883. Rather appropriately, the main decorative element of the building was put into the Upper Priory façade; the elevations to the yard were comparatively austere. The elevation to the street was three storeys high and three bays wide, with three small projecting timber gables above the three vertical lines of windows. The outer bays had coupled windows on each floor and the centre bay had a round-headed entrance opening, a single window at first-floor level and joined the other bays with coupled windows at second-floor level. The arched ground-floor windows had blind tympana, repeated at first-floor level as part of a richly decorated band across the whole front stretching from the first-floor arch springing to the second-floor sill. Above the second-floor windows there was timber panelling in the gables, or so it seems. To the right of the building there was an entrance to the yard, with a decorated, triangular panel over it, concealing the roof, and, to the side of the entrance, a heavy pier, with a pyramidal capping, supporting a large spherical light.

Eventually two problems emerged: the building was no longer large enough to fulfil its purpose, nor could it provide the rapid response needed for emergency calls, because of traffic congestion. A new building was erected on land between Corporation Street and Aston Street and opened in 1935, and it still remains the headquarters of the West Midlands Fire Service.

CHAPTER 3

THE COLMORE ESTATE

This chapter consists of a short perambulation through a comparatively small area, which contains many fine buildings. The walk starts at the corner of Edmund Street and Margaret Street. Proceed along Margaret Street, turn right at Cornwall Street and make a short detour to the left when you reach Newhall Street. Return to Cornwall Street and walk down the hill to Church Street and turn right. Proceed up Church Street to Edmund Street, turn right and return to the junction with Margaret Street. During this walk I shall refer to twenty-six buildings. Of these, eight were designed by one architectural practice, about which I will first say a little.

NEWTON & CHEATLE

It would be very easy to believe the architectural practice of Newton & Cheatle began in 1897 and ended with the death of Newton in January 1903, when he was forty years old, for all of the buildings for which the practice is known were built between 1897 and 1902. I felt this could not be correct and decided to find details of earlier work.

I had read in some biographical notes in *Birmingham Buildings*, by Bryan Little, that Thomas Walter Francis Newton was educated in Somerset and had been articled to Osborn & Reading, a noted Birmingham practice, and that's all I know about him with regard to the buildings from 1897 onwards. I looked in the records of building plan applications and the first references to submissions by T.W.F. Newton were for King's Norton and Northfield, in 1885, but the earliest of any significance were made in April and September 1887, for two and three houses respectively, in Park Hill, Moseley. The only other application I noted in the King's Norton records was for two houses in Main Road, West Heath, in 1892. I have made an effort to look at the drawings, which do exist, but they could not be opened fully because of their delicate state. From what I was able to see the designs were agreeable, but I would not go further than that.

The first reference I found for Birmingham was for a factory and house in Highgate Street, submitted in 1888, and I made notes of one application made in 1893 and three made in 1895 and saw some of the drawings, from which I gained nothing. The name of A.E. Cheatle appeared on the 1895 applications. Therefore, I shall limit myself to that work from 1897 onwards which does not appear later in this chapter, and which I consider to be worth mentioning.

There was another building on the Colmore Estate, erected in 1898, at 47–9 Church Street, for Buckler & Webb, but this has been demolished. There was an application in 1901 for a building on the corner of Edmund Street and Church Street, on behalf of H. Peery, but I have found nothing about it.

There were two applications for buildings in John Bright Street in 1899. One building has been demolished and the other application was made on behalf of an agent, so I do not know for certain to which building it relates.

Applications were made in 1900 and 1901 for factory premises in Constitution Hill, on behalf of Barker Brothers, nos 12, 14 and 16. I saw the drawings for this building and they show another building of quality.

In 1899 the practice was responsible for the rebuilding of the Fighting Cocks public house and two shops in Moseley, and I shall mention the building later in the chapter on public houses. There were also submissions for individual houses, pairs of houses and one for a new road and houses, adjoining the Fighting Cocks.

The largest scheme, although it came from several separate applications between 1899 and 1902, was for a series of buildings in New Street, stretching to High Street and Union Passage and incorporating the Midland and City Arcades. Nearly the whole complex was destroyed by bombing in 1941 and the area became part of the Big Top site. All that remains is part of City Arcade, leading from Union Passage, to give an indication of what was lost, and I shall refer to it later.

I believe that the early death of Newton was the most grievous blow that the architectural community suffered during this period, greater even than the early death of Chamberlain, for he was older, had accomplished more and the practice of Martin & Chamberlain continued to design buildings of a high standard, whereas I know of nothing of importance produced by the office of Newton & Cheatle after the death of Newton, although that may be due to my lack of knowledge and unfair to Cheatle.

THE BUILDINGS

The great advantage of starting from the corner of Edmund Street and Margaret Street is that the first building to be seen is one of the most outstanding in the city.

The College of Art, Margaret Street (see illustration on page 4), is generally considered to be John Henry Chamberlain's masterpiece. It may not have been the last building he designed, but his death, in October 1883, coincided almost exactly with the laying of the foundation stone. The college stretches between Edmund Street and Cornwall Street, with a short return to Edmund Street and a longer return to Cornwall Street, where an extension was carried out by the practice in 1893. All sides are worth seeing, but it is the frontage to Margaret Street which is the building's glory, dominated by three gables of different sizes and detail. The principal material is red brick, supplemented by terracotta, tile inlay and mosaic. There are too many things to see in this Venetian Gothic building for me to go into detail, although attention must be drawn to the magnificent rose window in the left gable. This is a building that must be seen and is deservedly Grade I listed.

Birmingham Library, Margaret Street, is now the Birmingham and Midland Institute and is on the opposite corner of Cornwall Street from the College of Art. It

The Birmingham Library, Margaret Street (now Birmingham and Midland Institute – B&MI).

was designed by Cossins & Peacock in 1899 and is Grade II* listed. The building is constructed of red brick with stone surrounds and has four gables of different sizes and detail.

95 Cornwall Street was designed by Newton & Cheatle in late 1900 for Smith Priestley. It is three storeys high, with an attic, and is three windows wide. It is built of stone up to first-floor window-sill level, with an entrance porch on the right side. The piers, from first-floor sill level to second-floor window-head level, are in brick, as is the parapet above the cornice, which is cut down to reveal the dormer windows. Sash windows are used at all levels. The building is Grade II* listed.

93 Cornwall Street. This is a slightly later building, of 1901–2, by Newton & Cheatle, for Sir James Sawyer and is Grade II* listed. This, again, is three storeys high, with an attic, and is three windows wide. The windows are sash type and the entrance is on the right. It is built of brick, with a plentiful supply of stone dressings. There are only two dormer windows that peer out from behind the attractive parapet.

Avert your eyes as you walk past 89 and 91 Cornwall Street, an attractive Grade II *listed building, for although it was designed by Bateman, & Bateman this was not until 1905. I am sorry you have to miss it.*

85 and 87 Cornwall Street was designed by Henman & Cooper in 1898–9 for Dr J.E. Parrott and is Grade II* listed. It is an unusual building of three storeys, with an attic, and has a narrow vertical line of symmetry rising from the entrance which dissolves into

85 and 87 Cornwall Street.

asymmetry to each side. There is too much to describe, and a special effort should be made to see this row of buildings.

50–2 Newhall Street, a Grade II listed building from about 1900, is on the corner of Cornwall Street, next door to 85 and 87. It is rather a sprawling building of red brick and stone, three storeys high, with an attic and a plentiful supply of features, which are distributed about the building with, I assume, more reason than rhyme.

54 Newhall Street was built in 1897 to the design of W. Henman for F.W. Richards and is Grade II listed. It is three storeys high, with an attic, built in red brick and stone. Its main features are bay windows in recessed panels at first-floor level and a porch that seems too heavy for the building.

56–60 Newhall Street is another Newton & Cheatle building of 1900, deservedly Grade II* listed, for it is a gem. It is four storeys high, with an attic storey, and is seven windows wide, built in red brick and terracotta. At each extreme there is a two-storey entrance porch with decorated shields above the doors. The windows at each floor level are detailed differently and there are bay windows on the third floor. There are gables above each outer set of three windows, with a chequerboard pattern in the apex.

43–51 Newhall Street. This building, known as Cornwall Buildings, is on the other side of Newhall Street and on the corner of Cornwall Street. It has three storeys and an attic and is built of red brick and terracotta, with four main bays, separated by minor

54 Newhall Street.

56–60 Newhall Street. *(Birmingham Central Library)*

41 and 43 Church Street.

bays, along the Newhall Street frontage. The outer bays project and the two main inner bays have oriel windows at first- and second-floor levels. The four main bays are surmounted by gables. There is a corner turret from first-floor level. Along Cornwall Street there are round-headed windows at ground-floor level above a semi-basement. The building of 1897 was designed by Essex, Nicol & Goodman and is Grade II listed.

53 and 55 Church Street was built as the Red Lion public house, but is now the Old Royal. I shall refer to it in more detail in the chapter on public houses.

41 and 43 Church Street is a Grade II* listed building of three storeys with a sub-basement, designed by Newton & Cheatle in 1900. It is three bays wide, with the outer bays having large bow windows with ogee heads, seemingly constricting or constricted by the centre bay. This bay houses a rather unusually detailed stone entrance, with a shallow bay window, at first-floor level, and a stone bay over it. The roof has broken segmental heads over the outer bays, separated by a dip, possibly modelled on a skipping rope. The building is better than my description would suggest.

37 and 39 Church Street is a restrained, Grade II listed, three-storey building with an attic, built in red brick and stone and designed by Newton & Cheatle in 1898. It is four bays wide, with the outer bays narrower and projected slightly. The outer bays contain the entrances, carried up to first-floor window-sill level, in stone.

158 Edmund Street, on the corner of Church Street, is a Grade II listed three-storey building, built in 1891 to the designs of J.W. Allen. The facing materials are brick and stone and there are three bays along Newhall Street and six along Church Street, joined together at a curved corner.

The Eye Hospital at 25 Church Street, now the Hotel du Vin, will be dealt with in the chapter on hospitals.

136 and 138 Edmund Street is a Venetian Gothic Grade II listed building dating from about 1880. It is four storeys high and five bays wide, built in brick and terracotta. The building has a strong vertical emphasis at first- and second-floor levels, where the three central windows are each sheltered within tall lancets rising through the two floors. This is reinforced at third-floor level by twelve windows, which are tall in relation to their width.

134 Edmund Street.

134 Edmund Street was built by Newton & Cheatle for G.J. Eveson in 1897, to an Arts and Crafts design. The Grade II listed building is three storeys high, with an attic, divided into three bays and faced with brick and terracotta. The central bay has rectangular windows at first- and second-floor levels and the side bays are recessed, with canted bay windows. There is blank arcading above the upper windows and a polygonal turret over the central bay. At first- and second-floor levels there are richly decorated bands of foliage.

133 Edmund Street is on the opposite side of the street, on the left going towards Margaret Street. There are not many buildings by Mansell & Mansell in the centre of Birmingham, but the standard of the few is high, as exemplified by this Grade II listed building of 1895, built for T.B. Scattergood. It is a three-storey building, with an attic, symmetrical above the ground floor, where there is an entrance on the right, with a broken segmental head. There are three windows at first- and second-floor levels, with panels above the upper windows reaching up to the cornice, which is surmounted by a parapet, broken by a dormer window.

125–31 Edmund Street. The practice of Newton & Cheatle was both architect and client for this attractive Grade II listed building of 1899. It is four storeys high and four bays wide linked, from first floor upwards, in the proportion 2:2. At ground-floor level there are four wide semicircular arches in stone that continue up to the first-floor window sills. There are four bay windows to the first and second floors, linked together in pairs above the second-floor window heads. At the third-floor level there are two wide windows in stone surrounds, with gables above which are decorated by ironwork features.

121 and 123 Edmund Street. Newton & Cheatle designed this Grade II listed building for G.J. Willetts in 1898. It is built in red brick and is three storeys high, with a dormer

125–31 Edmund Street.

98 Edmund Street.

window to the attic peeping out from behind the dipped parapet. At first- and second-floor levels there are three windows housed within a semi-circular arch the width of the building.

The Ear and Throat Hospital, 105 and 107 Edmund Street. This building has not been a hospital for some years now (see chapter 8).

17 and 19 Newhall Street and 103 Edmund Street. This magnificent Grade I listed corner building has a wealth of detail and ornament that would take too much space to describe adequately. The architect was Martin & Chamberlain (one of two buildings of the period attributed to Frederick Martin, the other being Spring Hill Library), and it was built in 1896 for the Bell Telephone Co. It is three storeys high, with a sub-basement and is faced in red brick and terracotta. It has to be seen.

27 and 29 Newhall Street and 106–10 Edmund Street. An application for offices and consulting rooms was made in 1894 by F.B. Osborn & Reading on behalf of W.M. Smythe. This is a four-storey Grade II listed building in red brick and terracotta, with a corner turret and gables.

100 and 102 Edmund Street, 44–8 Newhall Street and 78 Cornwall Street. These three buildings, all of 1875, have been gutted internally to form one office building, leaving only the façades. This building housed the offices of the Board of Guardians and was designed by W.H. Ward. It is built of stone to a French Renaissance design and is Grade II listed.

98 Edmund Street. Martin & Chamberlain designed this four-storey Grade II* listed building as offices for the Birmingham School Board. It is in the Gothic style and built of red brick, terracotta and stone. There are three bays, separated from each other by buttresses, each three windows wide (two at third-floor level), with piers between the windows in the wider central bay. A stone entrance in the centre bay supports a bay window at first-floor level. The window heads are different at each level and the double windows on the third floor are topped by gables with a roundel insert.

96 Edmund Street. This Grade II listed building was known as Empire House and was designed by F.B. Osborn. It is three storeys high and five bays wide, with the centre bay accentuated, built in brick and stone.

I hope this has not wearied you, for it is time to start the next walk.

CHAPTER 4

COLMORE ROW & VICTORIA SQUARE

The Colmore Estate covered a good number of buildings in a fairly small area. Our next tour covers a greater area and takes us into Temple Row, the upper part of Bennett's Hill, Waterloo Street and Temple Row West.

Great Western Arcade. This Grade II listed building connects Colmore Row and Temple Row and was built in 1875, the architect being W.H. Ward. The building was stone-faced. I say was, because the Colmore Row frontage has been changed beyond recognition. However, the Temple Row elevation remains as it was. It could be described as three storeys high, or two with a mezzanine to the ground floor; the latter may be more accurate, particularly as it is an arcade. The building is four bays wide, with the centre bays wider and the right centre bay containing the entrance. There are coupled Corinthian columns to each bay, leading up to a broad entablature at mezzanine level to three bays, with the other bay containing the semicircular-headed entrance to the arcade, with a carved panel reaching up to first-floor level. The coupled columns carry on to the first floor in the other bays, with windows at mezzanine level, with triangular pediments. The top floor is shallower, but plays its part in giving the building a ponderous appearance. The arcade is elegant, with a walkway to shops at mezzanine level. The arcade widens out at midway to form a circle with a dome, a feature that contributed to its listing.

Great Western Arcade – interior.

Grand Hotel, Colmore Row. The year 1875 was a popular one for buildings in this vicinity, but this time the architect was T. Plevins. There were later alterations and additions to Barwick Street and Church Street by Martin & Chamberlain in 1893, and an application for twenty-six bedrooms, in Barwick Street and Livery Street, was made by Henman & Cooper, in 1900. As befits a grand hotel, it is a large building, six storeys high, with attics, and five bays wide. The outer bays are five windows wide, with the centre window emphasised, and the other bays are four windows wide. The second and fourth bays are recessed up to fourth-floor level and then set back, with pedimented dormer windows to the sixth floor. The building is capped with a cornice and balustrade. There is considerable concern about the building, for it is in need of costly refurbishment and, although not a great building, is a very important part of the street scene in Colmore Row, as are the buildings between Church Street and Newhall Street, which form a very pleasing backdrop to St Philip's Cathedral and churchyard.

Since the above was written, the Grand Hotel has been listed Grade II*. Although I agree with the listing, I am very surprised it has received a starred rating, which I feel should be reserved for buildings of a higher architectural quality than the Grand Hotel. It must be appreciated, also, that the listing has not eased the owner's problems in finding a solution to the building's future. As the building's merit has now been publicly recognised, it is to be hoped that some public body will step in and work with the owner to find a sensible solution to ensuring the building's preservation and restoration for the long term.

55 (and 57) Colmore Row, 2, 4, 6 and 8 Church Street and 38 Barwick Street. This Grade II listed building, faced in stone and of indeterminate date, is similar to all

Grand Hotel, Colmore Row. *(Birmingham Central Library)*

of the buildings up to Newhall Street. This building, which is faced in stone, is four storeys high, with two attics, and has four windows to a curved return into Church Street. The entrance, with a pedimented head, is at the left side and the ground-floor windows have semi-circular heads and are set in banded rustication. The windows at each level are treated differently.

(59) and 61, 63 and 65, 67 (and 69) Colmore Row. These buildings, which were linked, although built at different times, have been gutted internally and rebuilt, except for the banking hall of nos 63 and 65. Photographs of the central building, which was the first of the row to be erected, taken soon after its completion, with earlier buildings remaining, show that the building line for the replacement buildings was set back several feet. This building of 1867 was designed by Yeoville Thomason, as were most of the buildings in the row. It is three storeys high, with an attic, and six bays wide. The centre four, above ground-floor level, are advanced and demarcated by wide Corinthian pilasters up to second-floor ceiling level. All openings have semi-circular heads and the ground floor has banded rustication, which is followed through in the side wings. The side wings, built at different times, the right one in 1873 and the left one later, are four storeys high, with an attic, and five bays wide, and are highlighted by a segmental pediment over the central first-floor window.

71–3 Colmore Row. Four storeys high and six bays wide, with semicircular-headed windows at ground- and first-floor levels and twin semicircular-headed windows to each bay at third-floor level. I believe this building has been gutted internally and redeveloped.

75–7 Colmore Row. This building is four storeys high and five bays wide, with the centre bay slightly advanced, with its first-floor window having a prominent segmental pediment to its head and a less prominent triangular pediment to the window head on the floor above. At third-floor level there are three triple semi-circular-headed windows.

79–83 Colmore Row. Another building by Yeoville Thomason, of 1885(?), three storeys high and five bays wide, with the centre three slightly advanced. The ground floor is rather crowded, with round-headed windows and entrances, including a prominent central porch. Over the first-floor windows there are segmental pediments and at the second floor there is an arcade of seven windows in the centre bays and busts of Benvenuto Cellini and Lorenzo Ghilberti, set in roundels, in the outer bays.

85–9 Colmore Row. From 1954 to 1958 I worked on the top floor of 95 Colmore Row and looked out on this building of 1869, known as the Union Club, and usually regarded as Yeoville Thomason's best building. It was a building of two storeys, three bays wide to Colmore Row, and the return, along Newhall Street, has four windows, the two faces being connected by a slightly recessed, rounded return. The right-hand bay to Colmore Row has a canted, stone bay window at ground-floor level, and the

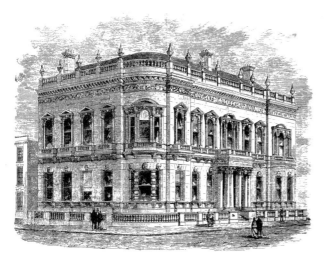

Union Club, 85–9 Colmore Row.

wide middle bay, of five windows at first-floor level, has a central entrance porch, with modern glazed openings to each side. There is a balustrade for the whole length of the building at first-floor level, which is repeated at roof level. There are triangular pediments to all single first-floor windows and the triple windows have segmental pediments. The building, which makes a fitting end to a pleasing row of buildings, has been extended vertically in recent years.

On a sad note, Frank B. Osborn visited the vicar of St Augustine's Church, Edgbaston, on Saturday morning, 6 April 1907, to discuss a new mission room. From there he went to the Union Club, of which he was a committee member, and, during luncheon, collapsed and died.

To continue our tour of Yeoville Thomason's buildings, we should now make a slight detour into Bennett's Hill, where on the left side stand

37–8 Bennett's Hill. These are two separate buildings, both dated 1868–70, of Italianate appearance, three storeys high and three bays wide. It is stated that Thomason designed no. 38, although on what basis I do not know, but I have no reason to query it, and, because of its similarities, he has been linked to no. 37. Both buildings are Grade II listed.

Please return to Colmore Row, turn left and proceed to

122–4 Colmore Row. It is most likely that the majority of people pass this building without giving it a second glance or thought, and yet I believe I am correct in saying that when there were only four Grade I listed buildings in Birmingham this was one of them, the others being the Town Hall, Aston Hall and New Hall, Sutton Coldfield. The building was designed by W.R. Lethaby, in association with J.L. Ball. Lethaby was one of the foremost teachers and writers on architecture at the turn of the twentieth century and had been chief assistant to Norman Shaw, but on his own he designed only about six buildings, including a house in Sutton Coldfield, which has been demolished, and this, the only one in an urban environment. It was built in 1900 for Eagle Insurance, is four storeys high, five bays wide and faced with stone and a small amount of brick. The central three bays of the high ground floor is filled with a large, mullioned and transomed window, while the outer bays have low entrance doorways with shallow hoods. There are string courses at first-, second- and third-floor levels,

122 and 124 Colmore Row.

separating the pilasters that divide the five sash windows at each level. Above the third-floor windows there is an extra-ordinary hood mould, alternately curved and triangular, and then a chequerboard pattern parapet, with applied, plain circular discs and, centrally, an eagle. The ground floor is currently occupied by Hudson, purveyor of light refreshments, and it is easy to gain entrance.

Council House and Museum and Art Gallery, Victoria Square. From an unrecognised building to one of the best known in Birmingham, the Grade II* listed Council House, which was designed by Yeoville Thomason and built between 1874 and 1879. It is faced in stone, three storeys high and five bays wide, facing Victoria Square, with the centre and outer bays advanced. Thomason put a lot of effort into the centre bay, with a portico, balcony, central arch, mosaic tympanum, triangular pediment and, behind, an undersized dome. The main features of the outer bays are attached Corinthian columns and segmental pediments. Around the left, curved corner there is the entrance to the Museum and Art Gallery, facing Chamberlain Square, added by Thomason in 1881–5. The entrance is at the top of several steps, under a two-storey-high portico, and is topped with a triangular pediment, with sculpture infilling. To the left is the clock tower, known as 'Big Brum'. You should go inside to see the galleries, Edwardian tea room and the exhibits.

Chamberlain Memorial, Chamberlain Square. Joseph Chamberlain had to wait until he was forty-four years old before the grateful citizens of Birmingham provided this memorial to commemorate his services to the city. It was built in 1881, to the design of John Henry Chamberlain, as a fountain with four gabled faces, pinnacles and a spire, and incorporating a bust of the great man. It is listed Grade II*.

Post Office, Victoria Square. The Grade II listed Post Office building is faced in stone, and was built in 1891 to designs of the architect Sir Henry Tanner. It is three storeys high, with an attic, and five bays wide to the front, with the centre and outer bays projecting and the outer bays at an angle. The outer bays have secondary entrances with pediments, and are capped with domed turrets. The more prominent central entrance also has a pediment and this bay has a pedimented attic. The slate roofs are steeply pitched. It is not a building I number among my favourites.

The Council House, Victoria Square.

8 Bennett's Hill.

It is now my intention to walk back along Waterloo Street, admiring the early nineteenth-century buildings on the left, and stopping at the building immediately before Bennett's Hill, on the right side.

11 Waterloo Street and 8 Bennett's Hill. This Grade II* listed building is a rebuilding in 1869, by John Gibson, of an 1833 building by C.R. Cockerell, the client being the National Provincial Bank. It is two storeys high, eight bays long to Waterloo Street and five bays to Bennett's Hill, joined together at the curved corner and housing an exquisite domed entrance. The bays are articulated by Corinthian pilasters, rising through both floors, and the ground-floor windows have semicircular heads. It is a most elegant building.

As you continue the walk along Waterloo Street, look at Thomas Rickman's building on the opposite lower corner of Bennett's Hill and stop at the junction with Temple Row West, where you will see the penultimate building of this group.

44 Waterloo Street.

44 Waterloo Street. The Temple Row West frontage of this five-storey building, with attic, gains from its open aspect, and so I will base my comments on this elevation. The building is faced in red brick and buff terracotta and its main feature is the polygonal corner turret, capped with a pointed slate roof, with the main entrance at its base. Next to this, at each level, are three windows, set between banded shafts, round-headed at ground-floor level, cross-type at first-, second- and third-floor levels and ogee-headed at the fourth. In the outer bay, set between banded shafts, are three light windows similar to those previously mentioned at ground-, first- and fourth-floor levels, and shallow oriel windows at the second and third. This bay is topped with a shaped gable, with a tall parapet between it and the turret. The detailing is good and Mansell & Mansell would have been proud of this very fine building when they handed it over to Ocean Assurance in 1900. Its quality is recognised by its Grade II listing.

4 Temple Row West. This is one of J.A. Chatwin's earlier buildings and one I like, although it did not pay much regard to its neighbours when it was built for the Birmingham Joint Stock Bank in 1862–4; but it has now been forgiven and awarded a Grade II listing. It is stucco-faced, two storeys high and five bays wide. The rather high ground floor is divided by an entablature, above which the windows terminate in semicircular heads. The first-floor windows also have semicircular heads and blind balconies between the columns that rise the full height of the building. The deep parapet terminates in a balcony.

4 Temple Row West.

CHAPTER 5

THE ORIGINAL BUILDINGS OF CORPORATION STREET

The Artisans' Dwellings Act of 1875 empowered towns with populations of more than 25,000 to buy property that was condemned and redevelop the land. This enabled Birmingham's mayor, Joseph Chamberlain, to raise once more a project he had first proposed in 1873 and which was to be known as the Birmingham Improvement Scheme. On 27 July 1875 he recommended the setting up of an Improvement Committee and stated 'it might run a great street, as broad as a Parisian Boulevard, from New Street to Aston Road; it might open up a street such as Birmingham had not got, and was almost stifling for the want of – for all the best streets were too narrow. The Council might demolish the houses on each side of the street, and let or sell the frontage land, and arrange for rebuilding workmen's houses behind, taking the best advantages of the sites, and building them in accordance with the latest sanitary knowledge.'

The area to be acquired was, in parts at least, in dreadful condition and at a Council meeting in October 1875 it was described by William White, who was to be Chairman of the Improvement Committee, as follows: 'In passing through such streets as Thomas Street, the back of Lichfield Street, and other parts indicated in the plan before the Council, little else is seen but bowing roofs, tottering chimneys, tumbledown and often disused shopping, heaps of bricks, broken windows and coarse, rough pavements, damp and sloppy. It is not easy to describe or imagine the dreary desolation which acre after acre of the very heart of the town presents to anyone who will take the trouble to visit it. In houses too, not of the worst class, but in the front streets, and inhabited by respectable and thriving tradesmen, intolerable structural evils abound. . . . In one case . . . the sitting room window could not be opened, owing to the horrible effluvia from a yawning midden just under it. If I were to repeat one hundred times "Dirt, damp, dilapidation", I should inadequately describe the condition of things.'

The centre of the Improvement Scheme was to be 'the great street', 22 yds wide, as described earlier by Chamberlain, flanked on each side by commercial properties, let on seventy-five-year leases. The scheme was approved unanimously in the Council, but was not looked upon so enthusiastically in all quarters, for many thought the town would be left with a mountainous debt.

The scheme approved by the Council involved the redevelopment of 43 acres of land and the cost was to be £1.3 million. The artisan population to be displaced numbered 13,538 and land had been purchased between Summer Lane and Newtown

Row for speculative house building. However, there were so many unlet properties in the area that none was built. At this time the Council had no powers to build houses, but only to acquire land for the purpose. The first council houses in Birmingham were not built until 1889, when twenty-two were constructed in Ryder Street, followed in 1891 by eighty-one in Lawrence Street.

The scheme was approved by Parliament in August 1876 and demolition work began at the New Street end in August 1878. By January 1882 the new street had reached Old Square. The architectural practice of Martin & Chamberlain was appointed Surveyor to the Improvement Scheme.

Although the construction of the street, to be known as Corporation Street, proceeded quickly, lettings were not taken up at the same rate. It was not until 1892 that a break-even point was reached; lettings were not completed until 1900. However, it did mean that all of the buildings were built in one generation, and this gave me the idea of trying to identify the original buildings and their architects.

Corporation Street is often looked upon as a great architectural opportunity wasted, and there were few buildings of great architectural merit. The majority were of average standard, which should be expected with many small commercial clients, but on the whole they were inoffensive and did not disturb the street pattern. Over half of the original buildings have been demolished, mainly in the 1950s and 1960s when the original leases expired, and I believe we have lost more by their demolition than we have gained by their replacements.

It has not been easy to identify many of the buildings, as there were more applications than buildings, there were never any building numbers and the owner was not identified on the application details until well into the 1890s. The biggest problem, as always, is that many of the drawings no longer exist or, in even more cases, the drawings are in such a fragile condition that they cannot be opened. I mention these problems to explain any omissions and, although I trust there are none, any errors.

THE BUILDINGS

I propose to go along the street in sequence, starting from New Street on the west (left-hand) side, going through to Steelhouse Lane, and then to come back and go along the east side to Aston Street. I shall break the walk into sections, going from street to street along the way. To most people, the street consisted of shops, rather than buildings, particularly from New Street to Lewis's, and so where there was a shop of particular significance to the typical shopper, or the untypical shopper as I shall fill the part, I shall mention it in relation to the building in which it was housed. I doubt that any of the shops I shall mention now remain.

I shall endeavour to give the street numbers as accurately as possible, but they do seem to have fluctuated from time to time and when I took photographs of the remaining buildings two were showing the same street number. Unless stated otherwise, the date, or the first date if more than one is shown, will indicate the year in which the building application was made.

Finally, before I start the review, a few general comments. Firstly, one of the most photographed sections of the street is taken from New Street and shows the buildings on the left side, more or less terminating at the Cobden Hotel. All of these buildings before the hotel remain, none of them are of great quality, but the whole make an acceptable street scene. Secondly, several very good buildings on the right side of the street, opposite Old Square, were demolished in the early 1960s. Thirdly, the best buildings are beyond Old Square and are very well worth visiting.

New Street to Fore Street

This section consists of five buildings. They have all survived to the present day, although the fifth is not the true original. However, in most cases this applies only to the façades.

Queen's Corner, on the corner of New Street, was designed to continue the lines of the Birmingham Daily Post Building, in New Street, around the corner, matching the cornices and semicircular-arched windows of the earlier building, although there were differences in the detailing. The application was made in 1879 and the architect was W.H. Ward.

Nos 3–7 combine to make another building of 1879 by W.H. Ward, known as Victoria Buildings. The building is five storeys high, with an attic, and five bays wide. There is a central entrance and contrasting treatment to the windows at first- and second-floor levels and to the head of the third-floor window. There are shallow, canted bay windows to the other bays at first- and second-floor levels, with pedimented heads, and the third-floor windows have scrolled pediments to the heads. The building is Grade II listed and faced with stone.

Nos 9–13 is another Grade II listed stone building of 1879, but the architect was Yeoville Thomason, who designed it for John Feeney, the proprietor of the *Birmingham Daily Post*. It is four storeys high and three bays wide, with canted bay windows at first- and second-floor levels, with decorated panels between. The roof has three rounded gables, topped with scrolled pediments.

Nos 15–17. The original application, made in 1880 by W.H. Ward, was for an arcade running through to Cannon Street, with nine shops and offices. A fire damaged the building in January 1888 and a new application was submitted in July, by Essex & Nichol (Oliver Essex had worked for W.H. Ward), on behalf of Central Restaurant public house. I do not know whether the fire affected the façade, which I rather like, but the influence of the arcade still shows. The building is of stone, has four storeys and an attic, and is three bays wide, the bays of unequal sizes and design. The main features are a circular oriel window at the second floor in the right-hand bay, above the arcade entrance, and a balustrade to the second-floor window in the left-hand bay, with a triangular pediment at the head. Yates's Wine Lodge was here for many years until recently.

Nos 19–23. Martin & Chamberlain made six applications for buildings in the early years, but I have only been able to relate them to four buildings, none of which survive today. This one, of 1880, for Marris & Norton, was the first to go, destroyed by the fire

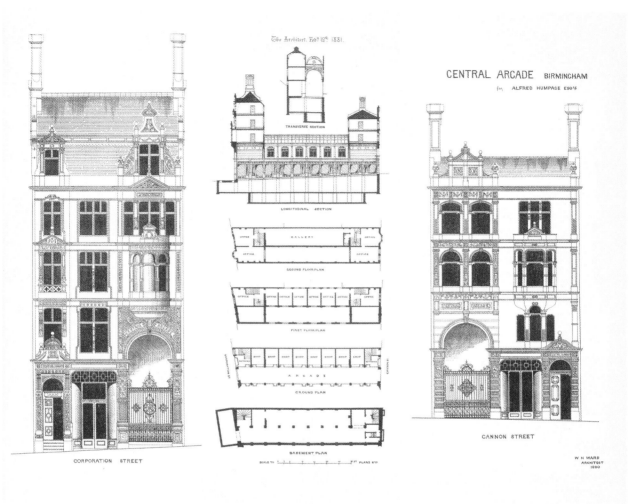

15 and 17 Central Arcade. *(Birmingham Central Library)*

of January 1888. A new application was submitted in July, by Osborn & Reading, on behalf of Capital & Counties Bank, which was to occupy no. 23. Norton & Co., the successor to Marris & Norton, was in the building in the 1890s. The main premises of W.H. Smith in Birmingham was at nos 19 and 21 for many years. The present building is of red brick and terracotta and four storeys high, with an attic. It is an untidy building, with, at roof level, a dumpy spire to a corner turret and gables.

Fore Street to Cherry Street
All of the original buildings in this section, none of great architectural merit, remain.

Nos 25–7. It is hard to distinguish this building of 1887 from the one next door, built in 1884. They were both designed by Dempster & Heaton, faced in a pinkish-red brick and stone, of unattractive proportions and details, yet they don't disturb the streetscape. There is a stone corner turret on no. 25, which was originally capped by an inelegant spire that was removed some years ago. The property was built for Pattison & Co. and was a well-known meeting and eating place for many years.

Nos 29–39. These premises, built in 1884, were owned by Clarence Property Co., when the offices were known (and possibly still are) as Clarence Chambers.

Nos 41–3. This building of 1883 was owned and occupied by the Midland Educational Co., a highly respected firm, well known to me and countless other Birmingham citizens. I not only visited the shop, but for two years sat at a drawing board in an office that looked out at the Cannon Street back of the building. It was designed by A.B. Phipson & Son, and faced with brick and stone. It has a symmetrical façade, in the proportions 1:3:1 and is the one I like most in this section. The shop is now occupied by H. Samuel, the jewellers.

Nos 45–9. This building, on the corner of Cherry Street, was owned by William G. Grenville, who presumably had a connection with the sports shop of that name that occupied the premises on the Cherry Street frontage. In the records of planning applications there are several in the name of Sharp, but not always with the same initials. The application for this building, made in 1887, was in the name of A.B. Sharp & Co. but I tend to give the credit to J.P. Sharp, although I do not consider there is a great deal to be gained from this building of red brick and stone. For many years the shop on the corner was occupied by Mansfield, the shoe people, in direct opposition to Dolcis, another shoe company, in the Cobden Hotel Building on the opposite corner of Cherry Street.

Cherry Street to Bull Street
All of the buildings in this row were demolished in the late 1950s to make way for redevelopment, most significant among them Rackham's department store. It may have improved facilities for shoppers, although some very good shops were lost, but among the buildings demolished were two that I liked:

Nos 53–7. This building, of 1882, designed by William Doubleday, was owned by the Birmingham Coffee House Co. and housed the Cobden Temperance Hotel. It was a vigorous, Gothic-style building, capped by an elegant, slim spire and was my favourite building between New Street and the Old Square.

Nos 59–79. Not the first or the last of the buildings designed by Dempster & Heaton, and not of the highest quality. I remember these premises, of 1884, more for the shop tenants than anything else, and these included Scotchers at nos 59 and 61, Bell & Co. at nos 63 and 65, Richards at no. 67 and Walter Austin at nos 71–9. The offices were known as Grosvenor Chambers, and Dempster & Heaton were among the tenants. The owner was William Ross, of whom more later.

Then came Bradford Passage

Nos 81–9. This building of 1882, designed by William Jenkins, was best known as North-Western Arcade, running through to Temple Row, and there is still an arcade in the same location. The firm of Wilkinson & Riddell was the owner and main occupier and the offices were known, appropriately enough, as Arcade Chambers. I remember, as a customer, Saxone, the purveyor of shoes, at 85 and 87. It was an attractive stone, Renaissance-style building, craving for symmetry, but foiled by the constraints of the site.

Nos 91–3. I cannot be certain, but believe this was a building designed by Dempster & Heaton in 1885. It was owned by Hall, Travers, Edge. In the early years the shop was occupied by Street & Co. and prior to its demolition the tenant was Timpson, the shoe retailer. I cannot remember the building and have only seen photographs taken at an acute angle, but it would seem to have been a symmetrical stone building, with projecting central bays at first- and second-floor levels, in a Renaissance style of not unpleasing design.

Nos 95–103. This building, Westminster Chambers, on the corner of Bull Street, was owned by William Ross, mentioned earlier, and the application was made by William Ross, Jr in 1882. The only people I have been able to discover with those names are a plasterer named William Ross and a builder and contractor named William Ross, Jr, operating in Small Heath. The building was one of the least distinguished in Corporation Street and might have been designed by the applicant, but if it was designed by an architect the only clue I can offer is that William Ross owned three buildings in Corporation Street, of which the other two were designed by Dempster & Heaton.

Bull Street to Old Square
Originally, there were three buildings in this section, but they were demolished in the 1920s to allow for the rebuilding and enlargement of Lewis's Ltd. They were:

Nos 105–13. The first Lewis's building was built on the corner of Bull Street, in 1885, and was designed by Yeoville Thomason. Joseph Chamberlain had invited David Lewis, who owned stores in the north of England, to open a similar one in Birmingham and, after investigation, Lewis decided that this was the best position. I cannot say whether it was the most important shop in Birmingham in its early days, but it was in my younger days and, in common with many others, I spent many hours in the original building's successor, which still stands, but not as Lewis's. The most prominent feature of the original building was a glazed, circular corner turret, rising through the six-storey building and its cornice from first-floor level, and capped with a dome. Along each frontage the three-windows-wide bays were separated by supports capped with tall pinnacles.

Nos 115–21. This building of 1885 was, as far as I know, the only building designed in the town centre by William Hale, a well-known local architect, and I would like to be able to describe it in some detail. However, the only photographs I have seen have been taken from a distance and at an oblique angle; so all I can say about it is that it had gables. The shop at nos 117 and 119 was occupied by the Cloth of Gold Agency (Liberty's).

Nos 123–9. Berlin House, as these premises were known, was on the corner of Old Square and stretched back to the Minories. The 1882 application was made by Kirk & Sons, an architect that I do not know, and the shop premises were occupied by Jevons & Mellor, hosier. The building was three storeys high, with an attic, in stone, with the main features at roof level. At the Corporation Street/Old Square corner there was a tower with a pyramidal spire over; and at the Old Square/Minories corner there was a domed feature. Next to the building housing Liberty's there was a squat spire.

Old Square to Newton Street

Nos 131–51. This site was the subject of what seems to have been an ambitious application, made in 1890, for an exhibition hall, hotel and three shops, made by J.P. Sharp & Co. *Kelly's Directory of 1892* refers to Birmingham Exhibition Hall, Winter Gardens & County Hotel Ltd, but, by 1896 this had become County Buildings and Wesleyan & General Assurance Society. In addition, there were several shops. In 1895 Ewen Harper submitted an application for alterations on behalf of the Society, which became the owner of the property. Later the Society moved to new premises in Steelhouse Lane, designed by Harper. For many years, before it was demolished, the building bore a large sign proclaiming 'Crane's Pianos'.

Nos 153–61. If I were asked to name my favourite of all the original buildings in the street I think this would be the one, which may be a little unfair to those I cannot remember and for which I have found no photographs. It was the subject of two applications, both made by Crouch & Butler on behalf of A.R. Dean. The first, in 1896, was for warehouse and offices and the second, submitted in 1897, was for business premises. The premises were occupied by Dean's, Furniture Manufacturers, and a vegetarian restaurant. Many years later, after he retired, Harry Parkes, the Aston Villa footballer, had a shop in the building. The offices are known as Murdoch Chambers and Pitman Chambers. The building is Grade II* listed, four storeys high, plus two attics, and faced with purple-red bricks and buff terracotta, and its colour is an important feature of the building. It is divided, unequally, into five bays of 1.2.1.1, looking from the street. The first bay has bay windows at the second- and third-floor levels, with a polygonal domed attic room over. The second and third bays are surmounted by a wide gable and there is a smaller gable over the fifth bay, flanked by squat attic turrets. In bay four there is a canted bay window. At first-floor level, over the three middle bays, there are three large, arched openings, with wide carved relief surrounds. Between ground- and first-floor level there is a deep carved relief band, running the whole length of the building. It is a building of great variety, which needs to be seen to be fully appreciated and is close to other buildings of quality, making the journey doubly worthwhile.

Nos 153–61 Corporation Street.

County Court. This is a two-storey Classical-style building of 1880, faced in stone, designed by James Williamson and Grade II listed. It is a very restrained building, keeping apart two very ebullient structures. The County Court and Court's Restaurant, on the other side of the street, were built some years before the other buildings at the northern end.

Newton Street to Steelhouse Lane

Victoria Law Courts. This is the most important building in Corporation Street and the only one to be Grade I listed. A competition to design the Law Courts was won by Sir Aston Webb and Ingress Bell in 1886 and the building constructed between 1887 and 1891, with an application for an extension being made in 1892. It was faced externally in red brick and red terracotta and its use of the latter was a revelation, both in the extent of its use and the quality of its detailing. The use of terracotta was not limited to the exterior, as it was also used extensively, in a lighter colour, in the magnificent great hall. This is one of the most influential buildings ever to have been erected in Birmingham and its construction brought joy to the faces of the manufacturers of terracotta.

Victoria Law Courts.

Then comes Coleridge Passage.

Nos 175 and 177. It would be very easy for Coleridge Chambers, as this building is known, to have an inferiority complex, situated as it is next to such a prestigious structure as the Victoria Law Court, but if it does, it hides it very well, for it is a fine building in its own right. It was designed in 1898 by J.W. Allen for the Birmingham Mutual and Sick Benefit and Old Age Society, and is Grade II listed. It is four storeys high, plus an attic, and is faced in red bricks and yellow terracotta. The building is three bays wide along each frontage, the bays being divided by polygonal shafts rising through the crowning gable. There is an arched central entrance on the Corporation Street frontage. At the corner, there is a polygonal turret rising from first-floor level, with a copper ogee capping.

Nos 175 and 177 Corporation Street.

Nos 179–203
Corporation
Street.

Nos 179–203. The street numbers show that this is a large building. Ruskin Buildings was designed by Ewen Harper, for Ewen Harper, and the application was submitted on the same day in 1899 that he submitted the building application for Central Hall, on the other side of the street. He and his successors practised from this building until the late 1960s, at least. The building is faced in red brick and yellow terracotta. It is five storeys high, plus an attic, and is thirteen bays wide. Each end bay is slightly advanced, and all of terracotta. From third-floor level the three central bays are divided from the rest by polygonal shafts, crowned with pinnacles, and are surmounted by a terracotta gable. The other two groups, each of four bays, are arcaded at fourth-floor level, with Ionic columns. There is much more to this Grade II listed building than this description conveys and it should, with its neighbours described above, be seen.

No 205. The last building on this side of the street covered by this survey was also designed by Ewen Harper, submitted eight months after its neighbour, but it bears no resemblance to its brother and I would have thought it was designed much later. I associate the building with the name Hawkins, but do not recollect ever having entered the premises.

We now return, walking along the east side of the street. The building on the corner of New Street remains, and then all have been replaced until we come to Lincoln's Inn Building (Gazette Buildings), beyond Old Square. From there, all buildings remain up to Ryder Street, and after that there are no buildings at all.

New Street to Union Street
Nos 2–12. This building is rather lonely, having lost all of its original companions and it is rather a pity that a better building was not chosen to represent all those that were demolished. It is called Prince's Chambers and was designed by Dempster & Heaton, in 1890, for Clarence Property Co.

Nos 14–20. This was an extension to Warwick House, of 25–30 New Street. The office section was called Warwick Chambers and the owner was Holliday, Son & Co. The first section, in New Street, was built in 1839 and the architect was W. Thomas, and it was extended later. It was an elegant, four-storey, Classical building and its destruction was a great loss to New Street. I believe that an application of 1880 for '4 shops and offices' made by Bland & Cossins refers to this building, for the practice was carrying out alterations to the interior at this time. The ground-floor premises were occupied by Holliday, Draper.

Nos 22–8. This building was completed by 1883, possibly earlier. The owner was Birmingham, District & Counties Banking Co. and the office portion was named Midland Chambers. The shop section was tenanted by The Don, and when I was young the name had changed to Thomas Donne, but the firm remained the same. The most likely application relating to this site is one made by W.H. Ward in 1879, but, having seen a sketch of the building, I would not recognise it as being by him and do not think he would have rushed to claim it.

Then comes Warwick Passage.

Nos 30–42. This building extended from Warwick Passage to Union Street. There were shops at ground-floor level and above these, on the Warwick Passage side, was the Victoria Temperance Hotel, not the place to stay if you wanted an en-suite bathroom. I have seen plans, but not elevations, for this building, and it seems that there was to have been a billiards club at the upper levels, on the Union Street side. In later years the building housed Lawrence's College. In 1894 William Denley was the tenant of no. 38, and he was still there in 1946, by which time England's were at nos 30 and 32 and nos 40 and 42. The building was owned by William Ross, also the owner of nos 59–79 and nos 95–103. The building application was made in 1886 by Dempster & Heaton and it was one of their better buildings in Corporation Street.

Union Street to Martineau Street

Nos 44–8. Prudential Buildings was owned by the Prudential Assurance Co. Ltd and the architect for this 1889 building was Alfred Waterhouse, who had been the assessor of the architectural competition for Victoria Law Courts and was one of the most distinguished architects of the time.

Martineau Street to Bull Street

Nos 52–72. This was a large development known as County Chambers, stretching down Martineau Street as well, and incorporating sixteen shops and offices. The architect was J.P. Sharp & Co., who moved into the building from 46 Cherry Street when it was completed. The building, of 1888, was owned by Corporation Street Estate Co. It was five storeys high along Corporation Street, but reduced in height as it went down Martineau Street. It was a worthy but unexciting building.

Nos 74–8. Lancaster Buildings was one of the first buildings to be erected in

Corporation Street, but to most people it was known as Barrow's, and it was owned by Barrow's Stores. I have fond memories of the place, for in the 1950s and early 1960s I lunched quite often in the dining room reserved for men. After the demolition of this building the store moved into a new building on the other side of Bull Street, but it was never the same again and no other store has replaced it. The building application was made in 1880 by T. Plevins, but I encountered some difficulty relating it to this site, for it was described as being for '5 shops and warehouse'.

Nos 80–6. This building was designed by Martin & Chamberlain in 1880 and was described as 'Premises for Avery's, Bull Street corner', which narrowed the field down as, from other information, this was the only possible site. However, by 1883 this building was referred to as 'W.B. Reynolds's Dining Rooms', and later, as 'Reynolds's London Restaurant', and I could find no drawings or photographs to help me. Then, I saw a reference in *Birmingham Faces and Places*, written in 1889, to looking along Corporation Street and seeing Barrow's and Avery's Restaurant. The building did not wait for the mass demolition but was rebuilt, it seems, between the wars and was occupied by Burton's, the tailors.

Bull Street to Lower Priory
Nos 90–102. This building was erected for A.R. Dean, house furnisher (see also nos 153–61), in 1885, and the architect was William Jenkins. The office section was named Dalton House and Dean's occupied the shop premises, nos 90–8. Later tenants included Halford and Dunn, the tailors. One thing has depressed me as I have done this research, and that is to realise how I failed to notice, or have forgotten, these buildings that were demolished more than forty years ago. It struck me most forcibly when I saw a perspective of this building and discovered that it must have had the biggest proportion of glazing to solid of any original building in Corporation Street. It was four storeys high, with a tall glazed ground floor, then two floors and a third floor, giving a vertical proportion of 2.2.1, capped with a cornice and balustrade. Along Corporation Street there were three bays, each three windows wide, followed by two bays, each with two windows. Along Bull Street there were three of the narrower bays. A circular turret projected above the roof line at the corner, capped with a cupola and slender spire.

Nos 104–8. These premises were owned by Central Buildings Co. Ltd and W. Hubard made the application in 1886. In the early years the upper floors were occupied by the Central Club and the application referred to the club, but later it became a YWCA Hostel. This was a four-storey, stone, Renaissance-style, symmetrical building, three bays wide, in the window proportion 3.2.3. The first- and second-floor windows were semicircular-headed and at third-floor level the number doubled in an arcade of semicircular-headed windows, with a pediment above the central bay. Kean & Scott was at nos 108–12 for many years.

Nos 110–12. This building was owned by Kean & Scott, but I have been unable to trace the architect. The choice seems to lie between Dempster & Heaton and R.G. Walthen, and applications they made respectively in 1885 and 1886.

Unfortunately the drawings are not available and I have been unable to find a photograph of the building.

Nos 114–16. Martin & Chamberlain made six applications for buildings in Corporation Street, but I have been able to find only four buildings resulting from their efforts all of which are now gone, one through fire and three by demolition, which is very sad for such an outstanding practice. This is one of them, built for Ray & Prosser in 1883, and it is the first of five fine buildings, in sequence, to have been demolished to the detriment of Corporation Street. (The last was, also, by Martin & Chamberlain.) Ray & Prosser remained in the building for the whole of its existence.

Nos 118. I have never seen a street number assigned to the Stork Hotel. I assume that it had one but considered itself too important to use it. It was another fine building that had the same use and name for the whole of its existence, starting from 1883. W.H. Ward was the architect for this very fine building, designed in a French Renaissance style. There were a few instances of Martin & Chamberlain buildings situated next to buildings by Ward, but there was never any danger of mistaking them, for Ward's were built in stone, in a Renaissance style, and the principal material used by Martin & Chamberlain was brick and the style was Gothic.

Lower Priory to Newton Street/James Watt Street
Nos 126–30. This building of 1886 was designed by F.B. Osborn & Reading on behalf of the Trustees of Central Hall, and the application was for Chapel Hall, shops and warehouse, but after a few years it was inadequate for its purpose and was replaced by Central Hall, built further along the street at the turn of the century.

In 1907 it began to show vaudeville entertainment; this changed by 1911 when it became a cinema, which continued until 1932. The building was known as King's Hall, even when the cinema was called Royal Cinema De Luxe. After the cinema was closed, the building became a market, and this powerful Gothic-style brick building was disfigured by the signs advertising 'King's Hall Market'.

Nos 132–48. This was another building designed by W.H. Ward, in 1883, I believe for Evan Thomas, and housing Old Square Chambers. However, its main function was to accommodate the Grand Theatre, the largest theatre in Birmingham at that time. People of my generation knew it as the Grand Casino, Birmingham's premier ballroom, when that meant something. It was an attractive French Renaissance-style building, of stone, marred slightly by the detailing of the upper part of the central bay, but its demolition was a sad loss to the city.

Nos 150–8. The owner and occupier of this 1880 building, one of the earliest in Corporation Street and designed by Martin & Chamberlain, was the Birmingham Household Supply Association Ltd, but in its last years the shop premises were occupied by Maple's, the furnishers. It was a three-gabled, Gothic-style brick building, with stone dressings.

Nos 160–78. At last we come to an original building that is still standing. It was called Lincoln's Inn Buildings when built, and comprised ten shops and offices. The architect was W.H. Ward, and the owner of this 1882 building was Evan Thomas, owner of nos 132–48. An application was made for extensions and alterations by Essex, Nicol & Goodman, in 1899, and I wonder whether Oliver Essex was involved in the earlier design of this building when he was in the employ of Ward. At some time the building's name was changed to Gazette Buildings.

No. 178. I was quite unaware of this building until I started taking photographs for this book, and I am unable to make any reasonable conjecture as to its origin. The shop is occupied by John's Fish Bar and the number is given as 178, and from here until Central Hall there is confusion with the numbers.

No. 180 (and 182?). This building was owned by Ind Coope & Co. Ltd and housed Central Restaurant and Court Chambers. I am fairly confident, but not certain, that this building was designed by W.H. Ward in 1882, and I would not be surprised if Oliver Essex was involved. The name of the restaurant was changed to County Restaurant after a few years; I assume that this change was connected with the opening of the Central Restaurant public house at nos 15 and 17, after the rebuilding of that address.

James Watt Street to Ryder Street
All of the buildings in this section remain.

No. 184. The Court Restaurant was built before the other buildings in this section, the architect, G.H. Rayner, submitting an application in 1882. It is now a Yates's Wine Lodge. It is a building of three storeys and an attic, built in brick and stone, giving neither pleasure nor offence.

Nos 186–90. This building, known as The Citadel, was designed by W.H. Ward in 1891 for the Salvation Army, as its headquarters. The building is four storeys high and stone faced. It is divided into five bays, symmetrical, except for a slight hiccup above the entrances in the outer bays. There is a pediment at third-floor level in the centre bay. Square towers with squat pinnacle rise above the roof line in the end bays, with a circular structure topped with a cupola rising from each.

Nos 192 and 194. In 1889 an application for two shops was made by W. Hawley Lloyd, on behalf of C. Cooper & Co. Ltd, who occupied no. 194 on its completion. The building was also occupied by the Law Courts Press. The building is five storeys high and divided into three bays, not too noticeable at the lower levels, in the proportion of 1.2.1, and is built in red brick and terracotta.

Nos 196–224. This project was designed by Ewen Harper and the application was submitted in 1899 for 'Central Hall, 15 Shops, Warehouse'. Central Hall is one of the most imposing buildings in the city centre and is deservedly Grade II* listed, and

Above, left: Nos 186–90 Corporation Street – The Citadel.

Above, right: Nos 192 and 194 Corporation Street.

Left: Nos 196–224 Corporation Street – Central Hall.

yet I feel a tinge of regret for what might have been. Just over a year earlier an application had been submitted to erect a theatre on this site, to be known as the Birmingham Alhambra, seating 2,400, with shops and market arcade. The applicant was Frank Matcham, the leading theatre architect of the day – and, probably, at any other time.

The main feature of Central Hall is its tall, elegant tower, which is a prominent feature on the Birmingham skyline. The building, of red brick and terracotta, is three storeys high and is five bays wide to the left of the tower, with small arched windows over tall oriel windows. There are seven bays to the taller section on the right of the tower, with tall semicircular-headed windows. At roof level there is a parapet with pinnacles and octagonal turrets at the end and corners. Its setting has gained from the loss of its immediate neighbours to the north.

Ryder Street to Vauxhall Street/Aston Street

The buildings in this final section have disappeared completely and have been replaced by roads and grass. The buildings in this group were generally of a comparatively small scale and erected in the last years of the original development. I have seen no photographs and can provide no information about the actual buildings:

Nos 242–6. The owners of this building were Sarah Anne and William A.J. Riley, but they never occupied the premises, so far as I know. I assume there was a connection with Riley who sold pianos at nos 30–2, 100–2, at some time, but do not recollect on what that assumption was based. The architect was J.G. Dunn, who made the application in 1898, with a further submission a year later to add a turret. The office section was called St Stel(l) Chambers. Lillywhite Froude was a tenant of 242 and 244 just after the Second World War.

Nos 248–52. This building was the subject of an application made in 1899, by J.P. Sharp & Co., for '5 Shops, Offices, Warehouses, etc., for Walmer Build (and Ryder Street)', although the owner was listed as T.C. Sharp, Sr. The property was known as Walmer Buildings and wrapped around 242–6 with a frontage to Ryder Street.

Nos 254–6. This building was designed in 1898 by D. Arkell, for R.C. Marsh and was for 'Two Shops. Offices and Warehouse'. Marsh was a jeweller at 18 Union Passage and 17 New Street, and I assume this property was an investment.

Nos 258–60. This application was made by J.P. Sharp(e) & Co. in 1898, for Birmingham House, Land & Investment Co., although the owner was listed as T.C. Sharp, who was a civil engineer practising at County Chambers, the building from which J.P. Sharp & Co. practised. Among the original tenants was the Corps of Commissionaires, and a later tenant of 260 was the Midland Bank.

Nos 262–4. Thomas Guest submitted an application in 1897 on behalf of Alfred Cooper, who occupied the shop premises and named the property Cooper Buildings. In later years the office section was called Unity Chambers and the tenants were mainly trade unions.

Nos 266–8. Albert Hunt, pawnbroker, was another owner-occupier, this building of 1896 being designed for him by R.F. Matthews.

Nos 270–4. The application was submitted in 1897 by J.T.(?) Sharp & Co., on behalf of Samuel Boddington, and was for three shops, presumably with offices above.

Nos 276 and 278. J. Gilman was the owner of these premises, for which an application was made by R.F. Matthews in 1894 comprising '2 Shops and Premises'. The site was next door to an existing building owned by Gilman, with frontages to Stafford Street and, probably, Vauxhall Street. I remember Gilman, a prominent firm of drysalters, on this corner, but have found no record of their occupying nos 276 and 278. At one time Harry Payne, boot and shoe repairers, had a branch at no. 276.

One application I have not mentioned was made by William Jenkins in 1898 and was for a horse trough. I think this would have been sited in the area of the Old Square. Only a lack of effort on my part has prevented me from establishing this as fact.

W.H. WARD

William Henry Ward designed more buildings in Corporation Street than any other architect, although manufacturers of facing bricks would not have been aware of this.

He was born in 1844 at Hamilton, in Scotland, and educated at Glasgow and Hereford. He was articled to James Cranston of Oxford and in 1865 came to Birmingham, where he practised as an architect in Paradise Street for more than fifty years. He was Past Provincial Grand Officer and Past Master of St James's Lodge. He had few equals as a shot and, as a young man, was the best heavyweight boxer in the Midlands. He was a keen cricketer and, on several occasions, was in the All England 22 team. He retired in 1914 in favour of his son, who had been his partner for some years, but returned when his son joined the services. He died on 15 March 1917, at 65 Sandon Road, leaving a widow, one son and two daughters.

In addition to the buildings in Corporation Street, there are references to buildings by Ward in the chapters on the Colmore Estate, Colmore Row and Victoria Square and hospitals. Much of his work in Birmingham was close to the city centre and among the most important were Colonnade Hotel, New Street and Ethel Street (1882), now demolished, and 48 New Street and Temple Street for J. and H.J. Creamer (1890), also demolished.

His practice was widespread, as this excerpt from his obituary shows: 'He designed infirmaries, workhouses and sanatoria in Cheltenham, Bradford, Brentford, Doncaster, Sheffield, Wolverhampton, Solihull, Alcester, Nottingham, Chesterfield and many other places. He restored Maxstoke Castle and parts of Warwick Castle. He built, or restored a number of churches. He built public markets in Mexico.' How did he obtain that commission in Mexico? He was an important architect in Birmingham and his best work was very good.

CHAPTER 6

NEW STREET & THE REST

This short tour starts at the top of New Street, goes as far as Stephenson Place, returns to Cannon Street, continues along Cannon Street to Cherry Street, crosses Corporation Street and finishes in Union Street.

At the top of New Street, on the right side, there is a block of four buildings between Pinfold Street and Ethel Street, all Grade II listed. The first three have been gutted internally and refurbished, and this may have had something to do with their listing, as I think the group is better than the individual constructions. The backs of all of them stretch through to Pinfold Street. All of them are noted as late nineteenth-century, but I have my doubts, as I shall explain when I come to the third. The buildings are:

80, 81, 82 and 83 New Street. This one is four storeys high and five bays wide, built in brick, with stone dressings. The windows in the second bay from the left are different at each level from the rest, and the fourth and fifth bays have been altered at third-floor level, presumably from necessity and not from choice. I remember, in particular, Dale Forty at no. 83.

84, 85, 86 and 87 New Street. This building is also four storeys high and five bays wide, but with a stucco finish. The second floor is prominent, with pairs of arched windows in each bay, each pair surmounted by a round-headed arch. At third-floor level there are groups of three windows in each bay, sitting on a decorated cornice.

88, 89, 90 and 91 New Street. Another building that is four storeys high and five bays wide, faced in brick, with stone dressings. The windows in the central bay are different from the others at each level. The reason for my doubt about the late nineteenth-century date for these buildings is based on this one, which housed the Masonic Hall. Photograph no. 77 in the book *Victorian and Edwardian Birmingham from Old Photographs*, by Dorothy McCulla, shows the laying of the foundation stone of the Masonic building in New Street, just below the RBSA building on the other side of the street, and the date given for the ceremony is September 1865. Older readers will remember that it used to house the Forum cinema. The architect was Edward Holmes.

80–93 New Street.

92 and 93 New Street and 3 and 5 Ethel Street. This building showed its originality by being only three storeys high, although it does have an attic. It is only three bays wide, possibly because Ethel Street got in the way, but it has a long return down Ethel Street to compensate.

From here we proceed down New Street to Stephenson Place, noticing, with some sadness, the deterioration of this section as far as being a shopping area is concerned, and arrive at the next building of the tour, on the corner of Stephenson Place.

128 New Street. This building, erected for the Midland Bank in 1867–9, was designed by Edward Holmes and is Grade II listed. It is stone faced, two storeys high, three bays wide to New Street, and the original structure was eight bays long facing Stephenson Place. At ground-floor level, round-headed windows are set in banded rustication in each bay, with the exception of the centre one to New Street. This houses the entrance, under a shallow porch, supported by twin Ionic columns up to an entablature and balcony, which continue around the building. The first-floor windows are similar to both elevations, but separated by coupled columns to New Street and single columns to Stephenson Place. The building is finished at roof level by an attractive entablature and balustrade. The property is now occupied by Waterstone's the booksellers, so there is no problem in gaining access to the inside of this fine building.

35–40 New Street. This building, opposite no. 128, was built in the 1870s, with an extension into Cannon Street in 1884, for the *Birmingham Post* and remained as a newspaper office for almost a century. The architect for this four-storey stone-faced building was Yeoville Thomason. The building is divided into three unequal bays along the front, with a curved corner leading into Cannon Street. The bay at the left is four windows wide and the other two bays each have six windows, those at first and second floors have semicircular heads and those at the third floor are segmental headed. The outer bays have a frieze at roof level, which raises the roof level above that of the centre bay.

35–40 New Street.

Among the shops I remember are Cornish Brothers at no. 37 and Hope Brothers at no. 40A.

43, 44 and 45 Cannon Street and 41, 42 and 42A New Street. Newton Chambers, the name of this building, was built in 1899, the architect was Essex, Nicol & Goodman and the building is Grade II listed. It is four storeys high, plus an attic, and faced in pink terracotta. The building is five bays along Cannon Street, the last bay being wider, different and containing the entrance. The corners to the New Street frontage are curved and capped with cupolas. In between there are four bays, the centre bays having canted bay windows at third and fourth-floor levels, capped with balustrades. Above there is an arcade of six semicircular-headed windows beneath a shaped gable containing a door and balcony, with pinnacles each side restraining the gable. The building was best known, to me at least, for containing the Kardomah, a popular meeting place and famed for its coffee, at least in the 1950s when I used to go there. The building has been recently refurbished.

39–42 Cannon Street and 9–15 Needless Alley. This four-storey high and four-bay-wide building, erected in 1900, is faced in pink terracotta, and I think it is safe to say that it was designed by Essex, Nicol & Goodman. The building follows the curve in Cannon Street. There are canted bay windows at first- and second-floor levels, with balustrades over, as on the New Street frontage of Newton Chambers. Above these there are twin round-headed windows below gables.

Continue to the top of Cannon Street and on the right corner of Cherry Street you will see:

17 Cannon Street and 10 Cherry Street. This Grade II listed building of 1881–2 was the first independent work of J.L. Ball, the collaborator with W.R. Lethaby on 122–4 Colmore Row. He played an important part in the architectural scene in Birmingham, both as an architect and educator, being the first Director of the School of Architecture. The building is deceptively simple, at first glance being a plain structure of red brick with timber windows, but when you look closely there are a lot of subtleties in the brickwork that are not obvious as they are not highlighted. In many cases there seems to be no reason for these details, and yet I am sure that Ball gave more attention to this building than was given to most buildings. One point to note, as an example, is the shallow, canted projection on the corner, rising from first-floor to third-floor sill level, which I find attractive, but it is hard to find the reason for it. Next time you are near this building stand and look at it carefully.

Now cross the road to Union Street and you will see:

City Arcade, Union Street to Union Passage. This is the surviving fragment of the Midland and City Arcades, which linked New Street, High Street and Union Street and were built at the turn of the twentieth century. All except this short length was destroyed by bombing in April 1941 and it was a sad loss to Birmingham's

architectural scene. The whole complex was built in phases by Newton & Cheatle, and this part is Grade II* listed and faced in red brick and terracotta. The main feature is the section incorporating the entrance to the arcade, which is three storeys high, plus an attic, and five bays wide. The arcade entrance is in the centre bay and rises through two floors, with a semicircular head. Above that, there is a narrow, five-light-wide window, then an elaborate frieze and cornice, topped with a shaped gable. To each side are canted bay windows at first- and second-floor levels, and these bays are topped with octagonal, domed towers. It is an exuberant façade, containing a wealth of detail.

City Arcade, Union Street.

CHAPTER 7

BOARD SCHOOLS & OTHERS

Before the passing of the Elementary Education Act of 1870 there were many schools in Birmingham, but they did not cater for the majority of children. According to the 1851 census only 35.5 per cent of Birmingham children between the ages of five and fourteen years were enrolled at a day school. Another survey in 1868–9 showed that the figure had increased to 39 per cent but this was distorted by the fact that 64 per cent of children aged from three to nine years were attending school. Up to that time the majority of children were taught at denominational schools, although this does not mean that other citizens, with interests of a secular nature, were not interested in educational matters. The first notable step forward had been the erection, in 1849, of the Birmingham Free Industrial School in Gem Street, designed by C.W. Orford. Under the Industrial Schools Act of 1866 it became a duly certified Industrial School in March 1868.

In 1850 an association was formed to campaign for the introduction of a free, secular and compulsory system of national education, supported by the rates, under the title of the Birmingham School Association. The Association achieved little of a tangible nature, but was involved in a series of national conferences. However, in 1867, at the instigation of George Dixon, then mayor of Birmingham, the Birmingham Education Society was formed. At the end of the year the Society provided the following information: 'The population was 343,948, there was school accommodation for 29,275 and attendance at school was 18,561.' At the annual meeting in April 1868 it was stated that 'There are now 80 schools on the list of the Society to which children are sent free. This comprises four-fifths of the whole number in Birmingham.' They attended free thanks to grants from the Society, which had received generous donations from many citizens.

In 1869 the National Education League was formed, with George Dixon again very much involved. The objects of the League were stated as follows:

1. Local authorities shall be compelled by law to see that sufficient school accommodation is provided for every child in their district.
2. The cost of founding and maintaining such schools as may be required shall be provided out of the local rates, supplemented by Governmental grants.
3. All schools aided by local rates shall be under the management of local authorities and subject to Government inspection.

4.   All schools aided by local rates shall be unsectarian.
5.   To all schools aided by local rates admission shall be free.
6.   School accommodation being provided, the State or the local authorities shall have power to compel the attendance of children of suitable age not otherwise receiving education.

To help achieve the objects of the League many people nationally and locally subscribed large sums of money. Pressure was applied to the Government throughout the country and this led to the passing of the Elementary Education Act of 1870. The Act empowered each district to elect a School Board with the responsibility of providing school places for each child in the district.

The Act did not satisfy the local Education Society, which had campaigned for free compulsory education for all children, with the intention of taking education out of the hands of denominational bodies. It gave School Boards the responsibility of providing school places only where these did not exist and these places were not free. A charge of 2*d* a week was made for children under seven years of age and 3*d* a week for older children. These charges, although later reduced to 1*d* a week, were not abolished until 1891.

Birmingham held the first elections for the School Board in November 1870. The Liberals attempted to secure the election of fifteen candidates, the total number on the Board, whereas the Conservatives attempted to elect only eight and in this they were successful. The Liberals learnt from this, and in the next elections, in 1873, fielded only eight candidates, who were elected. The elections in 1876 were uncontested. The chairman for the first term was Mr W.L. Sargeant and in 1873 he was succeeded by Joseph Chamberlain. In June 1876 George Dixon resigned his seat as MP and Joseph Chamberlain was elected, unopposed, as his successor. George Dixon then became Chairman of the School Board, a position he held for twenty years. At the first meeting of the School Board the firm of Martin & Chamberlain was appointed as Architect to the Board.

The Education Act of 1902 abolished School Boards and passed the responsibility for education to local authorities. By the end of 1902 the Birmingham School Board had built fifty-one new schools. I have made a list of these new schools showing the present use of the schools that remain. Almost all the schools were designed by Martin & Chamberlain, although those completed after 1900 were designed in the name of Martin & Martin, the new title of the practice. The only schools not designed by the practice were:

1888: Soho Road, designed by Thomason & Whitwell;
1889: Cromwell Street, designed by Cossins & Peacock;
1891: Burbury Street, designed by William Hale;
1901: Handsworth New Road, designed by Buckland & Farmer.

In addition to these new schools, Martin & Chamberlain made an application in 1876 for a school in Livery Street, but I assume this scheme was abandoned. Of the new schools, Waverley Road was a 7th standard school providing higher-grade education.

Oozells Street was converted to this standard in 1898 and renamed George Dixon Higher Grade School.

These are the new schools, listed in order of opening:

1873: Bloomsbury (Lingard Street), for 1,055 pupils. Demolished.
1873: Jenkins Street, for 1,136 pupils. Demolished.
1873: Farm Street, for 1,055 pupils. Demolished.
1873: Steward Street, for 1,055 pupils. Now BCMA Training.
1873: Garrison Lane, for 867 pupils. Now the Garrison Centre. Grade II listed.
1874: Elkington Street, for 983 pupils. Demolished.
1874: Lower Windsor Street, for 1,055 pupils. Demolished.
1875: Allcock Street, for 1,052 pupils. Demolished. Was Grade II listed.
1875: Rea Street South, for 1,070 pupils. Demolished.
1875: Osler Street, for 1,025 pupils. Demolished.
1876: Dartmouth Street, for 1,053 pupils. Demolished.
1876: Smith Street, for 972 pupils. Demolished.
1876: Bristol Street, for 1,023 pupils. Demolished.
1876: Nelson Street, for 971 pupils. Demolished.
1876: Norton Street, for 994 pupils. Demolished.
1877: Moseley Road (Chandos Road), for 1,017 pupils. Demolished.
1877: Fox Street, for 1,017 pupils. Demolished.
1877: Summer Lane, for 1,352 pupils. Demolished.
1877: Brookfields (Pitsford Street), for 1,018 pupils. Demolished.
1878: Oozells Street, for 807 pupils. Now the Ikon Gallery. Grade II listed.

Oozells Street – the Ikon Gallery.   Dudley Road – the Summerfield Centre.

1878: Dudley Road, for 1,220 pupils. Now the Summerfield Centre. Grade II listed.

1878: Little Green Lane, for 1,347 pupils. Now Wyndcliffe Infant School.

1879: Hutton Street (Eliot Street), for 1,095 pupils. Now Nechells Junior/Infant School.

1879: Montgomery Street, for 1,000 pupils. Now Montgomery Junior/Infant School.

1879: Dixon Road, for 998 pupils. Now Regent Park Junior/Infant School. Grade II listed.

1880: Hope Street, for 1,445 pupils. Demolished.

1883: Icknield Street, for 870 pupils. Grade II* listed.

1883: Foundry Road, for 1,002 pupils. Now Foundry Junior/Infant School.

1883: Loxton Street, for 1,095 pupils. Demolished.

1885: Ada Street, for 1,025 pupils. Now St Andrew's Junior/Infant School.

1885: Stratford Road, for 981 pupils. Now Ladypool School. Grade II* listed.

1885: Cowper Street, for 1,010 pupils. Demolished.

1887: Barford Road, for 1,080 pupils. Now Barford Primary School.

1888: Moseley Road (Highgate), for 1,116 pupils. Demolished.

1888: Soho Road (Benson Road), for 962 pupils. Now Benson Community School. Grade II listed.

1889: Oakley Road, for 1,110 pupils. Demolished, except for house.

1889: Cromwell Street, for 1,080 pupils. Now Cromwell Primary School.

1890: Camden Street, for 1,090 pupils. Demolished.

1891: Tilton Road, for 1,076 pupils. Grade II listed.

1891: Burbury Street (Farm Street), for 1,044 pupils. Demolished.

Hutton Street School in Eliot Street.

Icknield Street School.

Ladypool School, Stratford Road.

1891: Floodgate Street, for 1,115 pupils. Now Digbeth Centre, South Birmingham College. Grade II listed.

1892: Waverley Road, 7th standard, for 600 pupils. Now Small Heath School. Grade II* listed.

1894: Somerville Road, for 960 pupils. Now Somerville Primary School.

1895: City Road, for 1,040 pupils. Now City Road Junior/Infant School.

1896: Dennis Road, for 1,020 pupils. Now Anderton Park Junior/Infant School.

1898: Marlborough Road, for 1,065 pupils. Now Marlborough Infant School.

1900: Conway Road, for 1,000 pupils. Now Conway Junior/Infant School.

1901: Handsworth New Road, for 1,100 pupils. Grade II listed.

1901: Alum Rock Road, for 1,110 pupils. Now Shaw Hill Junior/Infant School.

1902: Station Road, Harborne, for 336 pupils. Now Harborne Junior/Infant School.

1902: Bordesley Green, for 1,038 pupils. Now Bordesley Green Junior/Infant School.

I have shown the pupil numbers on the list of schools, but should point out that having seen more than one list I have seen different figures for some schools and in those cases I have tended to go with the first figure found. The differences are not normally great, but with Elkington Street the figures were 983 and 780, with Nelson Street 971 and 800, and with Barford Road 1,080 and 1,180. It should be noted that, as far as I am concerned the figures shown were those at the date of opening, and nearly all schools had extensions and alterations that would have affected pupil numbers. As an indication of cost, the first twenty-four schools to be built housed a total of 25,239 pupils and the total amount expended on the purchase of sites and the erection of school buildings was £349,575 19*s* 1*d*.

The Board also adapted existing buildings, often schools, for use, sometimes of a temporary nature. The most significant of these were:

Park Street, opened in 1879, and **Meriden Street**, opened in 1883 as an overflow for Park Street. Both closed in 1891, on the opening of Floodgate Street.

Bridge Street 7th Standard Board School, opened in 1884, in a building rented from George Dixon, who paid for the cost of the necessary alterations. The school closed in 1898 after Oozells Street was converted to a higher-grade school.

Staniforth Street, opened in 1886 and accommodated 250 boys too badly clad for ordinary Board school. It was known as Staniforth Street (Boys' Free Order) Board School. It was closed in 1901 and the boys were transferred to Gem Street.

Gem Street, opened in 1888, the equivalent of Staniforth Street, but for girls.

Temporary schools, used until permanent schools (shown in brackets) were built, included Edward Street, 1874–6 (Nelson Street), Fox Street, 1874–7 (Fox Street), Brookfields, 1875–7 (Brookfields) and Benacre Street, 1887–9 (Moseley Road, Highgate).

The city boundaries were extended in 1891 and the following schools were taken over. From Aston School Board: Arden Road, Highfield Road and Ward End; from

King's Norton School Board: Clifton Road, Mary Street, Sherbourne Road and Tindal Street; from Harborne School Board: High Street. More information will be given about each of these schools when I come to its original School Board.

In most of the schools alterations and extensions took place during the time they were under the control of the School Board, and this applied also to the schools taken over in 1891 and some of those housed in existing buildings. The few that were built during the last few years of the School Board's existence had alterations and extensions ordered by the Education Committee. I think it is safe to say that none of the Board schools that remain look the same today as when they were first opened, and it is doubtful if they look as good as they did.

The practice of Martin & Chamberlain was appointed Architect to the Board in 1870 and held this position until it was terminated in January 1902, by which time the name had changed to Martin & Martin – as mentioned above. The practice not only designed nearly all of the new schools, but was responsible for almost all of the alterations and extensions to these schools and all others that came under the control of the School Board. The firm also designed the School Board offices at 98 Edmund Street, a building which is Grade II* listed.

In many ways the practice could have been looked on as the unofficial town, later city, architect, for it was responsible for the design of many public and semi-public buildings. In addition to the Board schools it designed the King Edward schools at Camp Hill, the magnificent College of Arts and Crafts in Margaret Street, and alterations and an extension to the School of Art in Vittoria Street. The practice designed libraries, including the Central Library and the attractive library at Spring Hill, Central Fire Station at Upper Priory, police stations, pumping stations, swimming baths, hospitals and the first council houses in Birmingham. It also acted as Surveyor for the Corporation Street Improvement Scheme.

H.T. Buckland was appointed to succeed Martin & Martin as Architect to the Board and was retained in that position by the Education Committee when it was formed. The practice of Buckland & Farmer was responsible for the next schools to be built and for the various extensions and alterations that were carried out. On a personal note, I met Buckland in 1942 when I offered to work for him, an offer he didn't take up and which, no doubt, he regretted afterwards.

In 1968 the local branch of the Victorian Society produced a booklet titled *The Best Building in the Neighbourhood*, referring to Birmingham Board schools. The Society was referring to the visual impact that these buildings had on the neighbourhood, rather than to the quality of the layout or the high standard of education provided. The fact that the Board retained the same practice as architect for over thirty years must indicate that all aspects of the service provided by Martin & Chamberlain were more than satisfactory for, in practical terms, the visual appearance may not have been so important as other considerations. These schools were recognised nationally for their quality, and I think this would not have been the case if they had failed to provide the facilities needed for the satisfactory performance of the function for which they were designed and at a reasonable cost. I emphasise this because my interest is in the visual appearance of these buildings and I find it easy to recognise them, in almost every case, as 'The Best Building in the Neighbourhood'.

Regrettably, a large number of these schools have been demolished and only twenty-seven of the original fifty-one remain, plus a house at Oakley Road, on the site of Holy Trinity RC School. Nineteen of the buildings are still in use as schools, and a few more are used for educational purposes. Icknield Street seemed to be in a rather sad state when I visited it, which is regrettable, for it is one of only three to be Grade II* listed. Seven other schools are Grade II listed, and so was Allcock Street, which has since been demolished. A school that has come out well is Oozells Street, which has been refurbished and is now the Ikon Gallery.

The design of the schools retained many similarities over the years, and possibly the most notable difference between the early and later schools was one of massing. Most of the early schools had a large proportion of the accommodation in two- and three-storey blocks, but I would think this was owing to site restrictions, rather than the preference of the architect, although it may not have been unwelcome. The later schools were largely single storey, although one of them, Floodgate Street, is entirely multi-storey and on a very restricted site.

The most constant features of the buildings were the main materials – facing bricks for the walls and plain tiles for the roofs. The roofs were a very important feature, being quite steeply pitched, with a proliferation of gables. A very early school, Steward Street, was the hardest to recognise, because of the shortage of gables, and was one of the two I liked least, the other being Station Road, Harborne, one of the last to be built.

Possibly the most notable feature of the schools was the tower, normally surmounted by a spire, which had a practical use as a ventilating shaft, in addition to being an important decorative feature. Each one was different and the best were extremely elegant. Unfortunately, a large number of the remaining schools have had their spires removed.

Another very important feature was the fenestration and treatment of the gables, and again the treatment was different in every case. To illustrate this, the *Birmingham Post*, in two different publications, showed the same photograph of a school, labelling it Waverley Road on the first occasion and Dennis Road on the second. When I photographed the schools still remaining I realised that it was neither of these, but Somerville Road. I was able to recognise it by the treatment of the windows and gables.

An attractive feature on some of the schools designed during J.H. Chamberlain's lifetime were wings with apsidal ends, used, even more appropriately, on the chapel at Rubery Hill Asylum.

Of the three remaining schools that were not designed by the Architect to the Board these features survive, but in the case of Soho Road (Benson Road) and Handsworth New Road, both listed, I think it is easy to tell that they were designed by other hands.

I have mentioned the two schools I like least and feel I should redress the balance by mentioning my favourites among those still standing. Of the early ones there are three, all multi-storey; in order of opening they are Oozells Street, Dudley Road and Icknield Street. Of the later ones there are Floodgate Street and Waverley Road, but I tend to think that I have picked the obvious ones, as all of them are listed. There are so many that I like that it would be easier to list those I do not consider worth a visit – which would make a very short list. I have left until last the one I like most, which is Ladypool School on Stratford Road. If you visit this you will have the additional pleasure, if you wish, of seeing St Agatha's Church, which is next door and is a Grade I listed building, designed by W.H. Bidlake, the only architect to have designed three Grade I listed buildings in Birmingham.

After H.T. Buckland was appointed Architect to the Board in 1902 there was a significant change in the appearance of the buildings, although the first new school he designed after his appointment, Oldknow Road, did not open until 1905 and was designed for the Education Committee.

By 1900 56,868 children were being educated in the schools controlled by the Birmingham School Board. In addition, there were School Boards in the following areas that were later incorporated into Birmingham: Aston, established 1875, with 12,518 pupils; King's Norton, established 1875, with 3,853 pupils; Yardley, established 1889, with 2,890 pupils; Handsworth, established 1892, numbers not given. There had been, also, the Harborne School Board, established in 1873, which covered the districts of Harborne and Smethwick. After Harborne was taken into Birmingham in 1891 the title of the Board was changed to Smethwick School Board.

ASTON SCHOOL BOARD

Aston School Board authorised the building of the first schools at a meeting on 19 September 1876, and during its existence built fifteen new schools and initiated the building of two others. They are listed below. There may be minor discrepancies in the dates in one or two cases:

1877: Arden Road, Saltley. Designed by William Jenkins, with extensions in 1884 and 1887–8. Now Adderley Primary School.

1878: Lozells Road. Designed by G.F. Hawkes. Demolished.

1878: Alma Street, for 1,023 pupils. Designed by William Jenkins. Demolished.

1878: Upper Thomas Street, for 1,003 pupils. Designed by William Jenkins, with extensions in 1885–6 for 300 pupils and altered in 1898. Demolished.

1878: Burlington Street, for 1,018 pupils. Designed by G.F. Hawkes, with extensions by Edward Holmes in 1889. Demolished.

1878: Vicarage Road, for 720 pupils. Designed by Edward Holmes, with extensions in 1880 for 510 pupils, and in 1881 and 1894. Demolished.

1878: Water Orton. Designed by Edward Holmes.

1879: Highfield Road, Saltley, for 350 pupils. Designed by William Jenkins. Now Highfield Junior/Infant School.

1881: Albert Road, for 1,102 pupils and including offices for the School Board. Designed by Edward Holmes, with extensions in 1885 for 318 pupils and in 1891. Now Prince Albert Junior/Infant School.

1882: Lozells Street. Designed by William Jenkins, with extensions in 1886. Demolished.

1885: Osborne Road, Erdington, for 470 pupils. Designed by William Henman, with extensions in 1898. Now Osborne Junior/Infant School.

1886: Aston Lane, for 1,008 pupils. Designed by Edward Holmes, with extensions in 1890. Demolished.

1894: Station Road, for 360 pupils. Designed by William Jenkins, with extensions in 1901 for another 600 pupils. Now Yew Tree School.

1894: Anglesey Street, for 406 pupils. Designed by C. Whitwell. Now Anglesey Infant School.

1900: Whitehead Road (Higher Grade), for 500 pupils. Designed by Crouch & Butler and Grade II listed. Now Broadway Lower School.

1904: Fentham Road, Erdington. Designed by Cossins, Peacock & Bewlay. Now King's Centre, Ashbourne Centre.

1904: Slade Road, Erdington, for 620 pupils. Designed by William Jenkins. Now Slade Junior/Infant School.

Albert Road School, Aston.

Whitehead Road School, Aston.

The last two schools were taken over by Warwickshire County Council on completion, as the School Board had been abolished, and in 1911 were taken over by Birmingham. As mentioned earlier, Arden Road and Highfield Road were taken into Birmingham in 1891, and of the others in the list above only Lozells Road and Water Orton were not taken over in 1911. I do not know what happened to Lozells Road.

Aston School Board also took over three existing schools. These were Gower Street, Ward End and Alfred Street. Gower Street was built in 1862 and taken over by the Board in 1876, was enlarged in the same year, the architect being G.F. Hawkes, and in 1880 had 1,128 pupils on the role. It came under the control of the Birmingham Education Committee in 1911, but has since been demolished. Ward End was transferred to the Board on 3 November 1879 and passed on to Birmingham School Board in 1891. I have not found any other information about it. Alfred Street was built in 1855–6 and enlarged and reorganised in 1882 after being taken over by the Board. It was extended again in 1889, the architect being William Jenkins. It was not transferred to Birmingham in 1911, and so I assume it had ceased to exist before that date.

There were, also, the following temporary schools under the control of Aston School Board: Erdington: opened in 1851–2, transferred to the Board in 1876 with 231 pupils, and closed in 1885 on the opening of Osborne Road; Villa Street: in use in the 1880s and early 1890s; Victoria Road: an existing building taken over in 1884 and closed in 1890; Station Road: opened in 1893 and closed in 1894 on the opening of a permanent school.

Seven architectural practices were commissioned to design the seventeen new schools, William Jenkins and Edward Holmes, with seven and four respectively, being the most favoured. In some cases competitions were held, including for Alma Street.

The Board decided that the winner of this competition would design Alma Street and one other school, and that the competitors coming second and third would also be appointed to design a school. This arrangement, presumably, left winners William Jenkins, G.F. Hawkes and Edward Holmes happy when the result was announced, but a letter of complaint was sent by others, and the signatories included Yeoville Thomason, Bland & Cossins and Bateman & Corser. It is interesting to note that some years later C. Whitwell (Thomason's successor) and Cossins, Peacock & Bewlay were each appointed to design a school.

The only school to be listed is Whitehead Road, the higher-grade school, designed by Crouch & Butler. It is more grandiose in appearance than the other schools, presumably to suit its senior status.

The schools were built mainly in facing bricks with plain tile, pitched roofs with prominent gables, as in Birmingham. This also applied to the schools built by the other local School Boards. I assume that this was the most sensible and economical way to design and build the schools, rather than as a result of the overwhelming influence of Martin & Chamberlain.

KING'S NORTON SCHOOL BOARD

King's Norton School Board built ten new schools during its existence, mostly during the early years. They were:

1876: Silver Street, Wythall, for 200 pupils. Designed by William Hale and extended in 1882.

1878: Mary Street, for 800 pupils. Designed by William Hale and extended in 1883 for another 410 pupils. Demolished.

1878: Pershore Road, King's Norton, for 453 pupils. Designed by William Hale and extended in 1882 and 1902, the latter by Edward Holmes. Now King's Norton Junior/Infant School.

1878: High Street, King's Heath, for 493 pupils. Designed by William Hale. The site was enlarged in 1890 and extensions were added in 1895 and 1900, both designed by Edward Holmes. Demolished.

1878: Clifton Road, for 868 pupils and with offices for the School Board. Designed by George Ingall and extended in 1883 for 310 pupils, and in 1885. Now Clifton Junior School.

1879: Stirchley Street, for 215 pupils. Designed by William Hale, with extensions in 1883 and 1893, both by Hale, and in 1896 by Edward Holmes. Now Stirchley Primary School.

1880: Tindal Street, for 813 pupils. Designed by George Ingall, with extensions in 1883 and 1902. Now Tindal Junior/Infant School.

1883: Rubery, for 154 pupils. Designed by Martin & Chamberlain.

1889: Sherbourne Road. Designed by William Hale and extended in 1891, when there were 1,462 pupils.

1900: Pershore Road, Cotteridge, for 615 pupils. Designed by Edward Holmes. Now Cotteridge Junior/Infant School.

Clifton Road School, Balsall Heath.

Tindall Street School, Balsall Heath.

Four of these schools, all in Balsall Heath, were taken over by Birmingham School Board when the city boundaries were extended in 1891. The schools were Mary Street, Clifton Road, Tindal Street and Sherbourne Road. The other schools, with the exception of Silver Street, were taken into the city when the boundaries were extended again, in 1911, together with other schools, built by King's Norton and Northfield UDC or taken over between the abolition of the School Board and 1911.

There were also at least four temporary Board schools, used for a short period of time until the permanent schools were erected. These, with the name of the permanent schools shown in brackets, were Balsall Heath Road, 1876–8 (Mary Street); Knutsford Street, 1876–8 (Mary Street); King's Norton Village, 1876–8 (King's Norton); Rubery, 1879–83 (Rubery).

William Hale was architect for most of the early schools, but I do not believe he held any official position, other than that he lived in King's Norton. In later years Edward Holmes, who was born in King's Heath, was more favoured, although by that time his son, Teddie, may have been playing a more prominent part. Of some interest, William Hale came to Birmingham to be chief assistant in the practice of Edward Holmes. I assume Martin & Chamberlain was appointed to design the school at Rubery because it was adjacent to Rubery Hill Asylum, for which the practice was architect and which was being built at that time.

None of the schools is listed and neither are any of those built later by King's Norton and Northfield UDC.

Yardley School Board

During its comparatively brief existence Yardley School Board was responsible for the erection of six new schools. They came under the control of Worcestershire County Council after the abolition of the School Board and were taken over by the city in 1911, together with four schools erected between 1907 and 1910. The Board schools were:

1892: Warwick Road, Greet, for 1,035 pupils. Designed by Arthur Harrison. Now Greet Junior School.

1892: Redhill Road, Hay Mills, for 540 pupils. Designed by Crouch & Butler, with an extension in 1894, for 428 pupils. Now Redhill Primary School.

1893: School Road, Yardley Wood, for 251 pupils. Designed by Arthur Harrison. Now Yardley Wood Primary School.

1893: Stratford Road, Hall Green, for 240 pupils. Designed by Arthur Harrison. Now Hall Green Junior/Infant School.

1896: Albert Road, Stechford, for 396 pupils. Designed by R.F. Matthews. Now Stechford Junior/Infant School.

1900: College Road, Moseley, for 1,130 pupils. Designed by R.F. Matthews. Now Springfield Junior/Infant School.

There were also three temporary Board schools, which closed when the permanent schools (shown in brackets) opened: Bard Street, 1890–2 (Warwick Road); Hall Green, 1890–3 (Hall Green); Rushall Lane, 1891–2 (Redhill Road).

Warwick Road School, Greet. *(Birmingham Central Library)*

Competitions were held to select the architect for the first two schools and the last one. Arthur Harrison was chosen to design the School Board offices, a commission perhaps, not so prestigious as it sounds, for I have seen a contract figure of £678. However, it's the thought that counts.

HANDSWORTH SCHOOL BOARD

During its short existence Handsworth School Board built four new schools, which are listed below. An existing school, Boulton Road, which is still in use, is also included in the list:

1884: Boulton Road opened in 1884 and was taken over by the School Board in 1892. Alterations were carried out in 1893, by J.R. Nicholls, then extensions in 1896, including a caretaker's house by A.E. McKewan, and further extensions in 1901, by Wood & Kendrick. Now Boulton Junior/Infant School.

1895: Wattville Street (Road in 1912), for 1,056 pupils. Designed by Wood & Kendrick and extended in 1900–1 for another 540 pupils, by the same practice. Now Wattville Junior School.

1895: Birchfield Road, for 660 pupils. Designed by J.P. Osborne, with an extension to complete the original design in 1896. Demolished.

1899: Rookery Road, for 1,060 pupils. Designed by Edward Holmes and Grade II listed. Now Rookery Junior/Infant School.

1903: Grove Lane, for 1,010 pupils. Designed by Wood & Kendrick and Grade II listed. Now Grove Junior/Infant School.

For a very short period there was Christchurch Board School, opened in 1874, transferred to the Board in 1894 and closed in 1895.

Wood & Kendrick was appointed to design Board offices, a pupil teachers' centre and a caretaker's house at the Portland House site, Soho Hill, and instructions were given to proceed in June 1902. It is hoped that the Board was able to make some use of the building before its last meeting, on 26 June 1903.

Competitions were held to choose the architect for each of the new schools, with the exception of Grove Lane. Two of the schools are listed buildings, as is Canterbury Road, opened in 1907. I had never heard of J.R. Nicholls before seeing his commission for Boulton Road, which hardly seems prestigious and did not lead to better things, at least as far as Handsworth School Board was concerned. The five schools, together with another two built later, were taken into Birmingham in 1911.

HARBORNE SCHOOL BOARD

As mentioned earlier, Harborne School Board was formed in 1873 and changed its name to Smethwick School Board when Harborne was incorporated into Birmingham in 1891. This would always have seemed to be the more logical title, for the Board offices were located in Cross Street, Smethwick, and nearly all of the new schools were built in Smethwick.

The only new school in Harborne was built on what is now High Street and was erected in 1881. It is now used as a further education centre and is known as the Clock Tower. It is Grade II listed. The building was designed by J.P. Sharp & Co., who had been appointed as Architect to the Board in April 1874, receiving five votes as against the four cast for R. Phipson, who had also been nominated.

CONCLUSIONS

In the just over thirty years of School Boards a total of eighty-seven new Board schools were opened in the area covered by present-day Birmingham. Two others were built

High Street, Harborne – the Clock Tower.

outside the present city boundaries: Silver Street, Wythall, and Water Orton. In addition, several existing schools were taken over, improved and enlarged. This was a tremendous undertaking, carried out with great conscientiousness by civic-minded citizens. Birmingham School Board acted so efficiently in discharging its duties that very few new schools had to be built in the area that it had covered in the period from its abolition up to the First World War. The schools provided educational places for about 90,000 pupils by 1903 and, in addition, enhanced the neighbourhoods where they were sited through their appearance.

OTHER SCHOOLS & COLLEGES

This is a comparatively small selection, but, hopefully, of some interest. I intended, originally, to include three of the colleges in the section on Religious Buildings, but, after some deliberation, decided that the educational aspect was more important. I would agree that not to include in this section the most prestigious building, the College of Art in Margaret Street, may be considered perverse, but I am here to make decisions, even if not equal to the task. I shall deal with the buildings in the order they were built, which means that two of the colleges referred to above will take first and second places.

St Peter's College, College Walk, Saltley was built in 1847–52, the architect was Benjamin Ferry and it is Grade II listed. The college was built in the Tudor style around a quadrangle, with buildings two storeys high, plus an attic, to three sides, although not all of the same height, and with towers at the internal corners. There is a gable to the entrance, with an oriel window over, on the exterior face. The finish is rock-faced ironstone, with sandstone dressings. There have been various additions over the years, and when I went on an arranged visit a few years ago the buildings were being put to various uses by a variety of firms and organisations.

Spring Hill Congregational College, Wake Green Road, Moseley. The college was founded by a family named Mansfield and was built in a Decorated style by Joseph

Spring Hill Congregational College, Wake Green Road.

James in 1855–6, and is Grade II listed. The facing material is red brick, with stone dressings. It is not an easy building to describe simply and briefly, for there is so much going on, seemingly at many levels. The main feature of the entrance front is the tower containing the entrance, with a two-storey oriel window over and a corner turret and crenellated top. The college moved to Oxford in the 1880s, where it became Mansfield College. After being put to other uses the building reverted to being an educational establishment in 1923, when it became Moseley Boys' Grammar School, and I believe it is now a part of Moseley School.

St Philip's Grammar School, Hagley Road, Edgbaston was built in 1859–61, the architect was Henry Clutton and the building, on the road front, is Grade II* listed. This block is faced in red brick, with stone dressings, and is two storeys high and six bays long. The windows, at first-floor level, are arched casements, in stone surrounds, sitting on a string course. The building is topped with an eaves cornice and parapet. An entrance from the front leads through a vaulted passage to a cloistered courtyard.

Handsworth Grammar School, Grove Lane, Handsworth. This building was designed by George Bidlake, the father of W.H. Bidlake, and was opened in 1862 as the Bridge Trust School, and comprised main room, two classrooms and a boardroom. It became Handsworth Grammar School in about 1890. There have been additions over the years, but the Grade II listing is limited to this building. The facing materials are red and black bricks and stone dressings, and the roof is tiled. It is a single storey, seven bays long, the first, sixth and seventh being advanced and all being gabled, except for the sixth, which contains the entrance. Additionally, it is a clock tower and has an unusual, or ungainly, bell turret over. The seventh bay has a central, tall, three-light window and two lancet-type windows. Bays two to five accommodate the main room, and each has a three-light window. There is a shingled louvred turret on the ridge.

Branch School of Art, 82, 84 and 86 Vittoria Street. This is now the School of Jewellery and consists of three main units: from the left, viewed from the street, an extension of 1992–3, an extension of 1911 and the original building of 1865. This was a two-storey Venetian Gothic building, designed by J.G. Bland as a jeweller's workshop and office. The facing materials are red brick, with stone dressings and tile work. The windows are set in arches with brick and stone gauged work. The building was adapted in 1890 to become a branch school of art and additions were made in 1900, both commissions being carried out by Martin & Chamberlain. The building is Grade II listed.

Town School, Mill Street, Sutton Coldfield. The school was founded in 1825 with the purpose of providing 'the moral and religious instruction of 50 male and 50 female children of the poor inhabitants'. An addition to the school was built in 1870, but sanitary conditions were so bad that there were outbreaks of illness and the school was closed for three months in 1876. Other enlargements took place in 1888 and 1902 and a new school for 450 boys was opened on an adjoining site in Victoria Road in 1907. The figures I have seen for pupils at the original school were 356 girls and 128 infants.

Bridge Trust School, Grove Lane, Handsworth. *(Birmingham Central Library)*

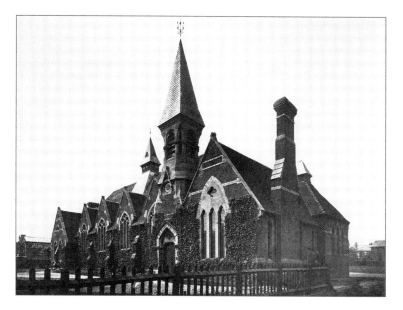

Town School, Mill Street, Sutton Coldfield.

The 1870 Gothic-style school faced, and still faces, Lower Parade, and the main, taller section comprises six gabled bays of brick, with stone dressings, with tall arched windows at the upper level and arched openings below. The buildings ceased to be a school some years ago and are now the home of Sutton Coldfield Baptist church.

Methodist Theological College, Friary Road, Handsworth. Goddard & Ball won a competition to design this college in 1881 and J.L. Ball then came to Birmingham and began his own practice. The main front of the building has nine two-storey bays on each side of a four-storey tower, with a deep parapet and polygonal turrets with cupolas. The tower houses the main entrance and, above it, there is a two-storey oriel window. The building is of brick, with purple diaper and buff terracotta dressings. The building is now known as Handsworth Hall, is part of Aston University and is Grade II listed.

King Edward VI Grammar School, Frederick Road, Aston. The school was erected in 1883 to accommodate boys and girls and was designed by J.A. Chatwin. Two two-storey wings, each providing an assembly hall, nine classrooms and ancillary accommodation, were built at right angles to Frederick Road at the two extremities of the site, one for the boys and the other for the girls. The wings extended through to Albert Road at the rear. A single-storey wing was constructed along the Frederick Street frontage, containing the separate entrances and the caretaker's house, and an upper floor was added to this in 1896. The wings are two bays wide and gabled and the inner bays are slightly shorter in length. The outer bays, at each end, have wide, two-storey, canted bay windows, crowned with crenellations. The inner bays of the central section, facing the courtyard, are wider and higher, and comprise six bays separated by buttresses terminating at the springing of the arches of the first-floor windows. The principal material is red brick with terracotta dressings. In 1911 the girls transferred to a new building in Rosehill Road, Handsworth. The Aston site is the only one of those in use in 1883 to be still used for its original purpose by the King Edward's Foundation.

King Edward VI Grammar School, Camp Hill. The school has later additions, but I am concerned only with the first two buildings: viewed from the road, that for the boys, built in 1883, on the left side, and the building for the girls, erected in 1891–2, on the right side. Both buildings were designed by Martin & Chamberlain and are Grade II listed. The school moved to new premises in King's Heath some years ago and this site is now the Bordesley Centre. The buildings are two storeys high, built in red brick, with stone and terracotta dressings and the roofs are tiled. At the north (left) end of the earlier building there is a bowed, arcaded base projecting from a tower, which becomes an octagonal turret, then a timber-framed section, and terminates with

King Edward VI Grammar School for Boys, Camp Hill. *(Birmingham Central Library)*

College of Art, Moseley Road.

a slate spire. Behind the tower there is a gabled end, with a wide, five-light window. The windows to the front are coupled and triple lancet and there are two gables of differeing heights. At the rear there are three gables to the main block, each with triple windows in typical Board school style. To the right there is a projecting block, with splayed corners and a hipped roof. The main block of the later building is six bays wide, separated by buttresses, with twin-arched windows to each bay at ground-floor level and four bays at first-floor. There is a gable to the two centre bays, with larger first-floor windows and a rose window over. To the right there is a projecting gable wing.

College of Art, Moseley Road. Described as a 'Wrenaissance' design, this Grade II* listed building of 1899 was designed by W.H. Bidlake. It is two storeys high, with a semi-basement, and is seven bays wide. The front is dominated by the central two-storey stone portico, sheltering the entrance at ground-floor level and protecting a shallow bay window at the first floor, with its Doric columns and open segmental pediment. The string course of the first-floor entablature continues along the other bays supporting the engaged columns between the first-floor windows. The narrow ground-floor windows in their stone surrounds look rather mean and out of place to me. The principal materials are red brick and stone and the roof is slate, swept down to the eaves. The building looked in a run-down condition when I last saw it, in about 2000.

CHAPTER 8

HOSPITALS

The first hospital built in Birmingham, with the exception of the Workhouse Infirmary, was the **General Hospital** in Summer Lane, built between 1766 and 1779 on the initiative of John Ash, a local physician, and financed by various fund-raising efforts. It remained there, with extensions, including the addition of a wing designed in 1857 by William Martin and nurses' homes and burns wards by Yeoville Thomason in 1880, until the new General Hospital opened in Steelhouse Lane in 1897. The site in Summer Lane was subsequently occupied by a power station.

The design for the new hospital was decided by competition, and was won by William Henman in 1892. *The Builder* noted that 'Architectural effect has been combined with practical arrangement and construction more completely and successfully than is usual in large hospital buildings.' It is built in red brick and red terracotta, of a Renaissance design, and I think is rather better than its press of recent years would suggest, although it has suffered over the years from some unfortunate extensions. It is now the Diana, Princess of Wales Children's Hospital, and able to look forward to a bright future.

Queen's Hospital in Bath Row, the next hospital of interest to me, was the brainchild of a local surgeon, W. Sands Cox, and funded by local subscription. The first building, the east block, was designed by Bateman & Drury in 1840. It is a three-storey, late Regency building, three bays wide, in the proportion 2.3.2, with the centre bay recessed. The building is faced with stone up to first-floor level, with red brick above. This Grade II listed building has a shallow, stone entrance porch.

General Hospital, Steelhouse Lane.
(Birmingham Central Library)

The west block, also Grade II listed, was added in 1873, by Martin & Chamberlain. It is a most unusual, but interesting, building for this practice, for it is Italianate in style, two storeys high, with a raised, pedimented centre. The facing materials are red brick and ashlar dressings, and it has entablature and a parapet to the roof and central portico.

The hospital later became the Accident Hospital, but this function ceased in 1993.

Borough Lunatic Asylum opened in 1849, in Lodge Road, Winson Green, next door to the prison. Both were designed by D.R. Hill, but not in the same style. The Asylum is a Tudor-style building, faced in red brick, with stone dressings, and is divided into five main bays, with the centre and outside bays being subdivided into minor bays. The centre and outside bays are three storeys high and the separating bays are two storeys high and all have a sub-basement. The centre bay is divided into five minor bays, with the entrance in the centre, above which is a two-storey, canted bay window, with a balustrade over which continues over the adjacent minor bays. The outside minor bays are advanced and crowned with shaped gables, which are matched on the centre, advanced, minor bays of the outside main bays, which I hope does not seem too complicated. There is a continuous decorated band running the length of the building at first-floor level.

There were several extensions carried out in the Victorian period. The first, by William Martin, added four three-storey blocks, comprising eight day rooms, with dormitories over. The next, in 1878, added a large dormitory accommodating fifty beds and the last, in 1888, involved alterations and additions to no. 8 ward, both of these projects by Martin & Chamberlain.

All of this became All Saints' Hospital and is Grade II listed, but its use as a hospital ceased and I believe a new use is being sought.

The Birmingham Union Workhouse was moved from Lichfield Street to a site in Western Road, Winson Green, in 1851, to a building designed by J.J. Bateman. It was a large complex, designed initially to house 1,100 inmates, but the numbers increased significantly. The building was designed in a Tudor style around courtyards separating

Queen's Hospital, Bath Row. *(Birmingham Central Library)*

the different groups into Infants, Girls, Boys, Probationary Children, Infirm Women, Infirm Men, Disorderly Women, Disorderly Men, Able Women, Able Men, Female Tramps, Male Tramps, Female Probationers and Male Probationers. Please do not say there wasn't a category for you.

Many of the inmates were there because of age and/or illness and sick wards were needed. So, in 1889 a Workhouse Infirmary was added, with nine wards or pavilions, linked by a corridor a quarter of a mile long, containing a total of 1,100 beds. The architect was W.H. Ward.

These buildings eventually became part of Dudley Road Hospital, which in due course changed its name to City Hospital, and although most of the workhouse has gone the infirmary has done rather better.

Highcroft Hospital, Highcroft Road, was built originally as the Aston Union Workhouse to replace a building that had become overcrowded, facing Erdington Village Green. The workhouse was built between 1865 and 1871 to accommodate 250 children and 250 adults, but in a few years the numbers had increased appreciably. The original building is three storeys high, with a taller central block and a lantern tower. The main building and the entrance front range have been Grade II listed and the site is being gradually redeveloped. The architect was Yeoville Thomason.

The Birmingham and Midland Free Hospital for Sick Children was established in 1861 by Dr Thomas Heslop in premises in Steelhouse Lane, formerly used by the Polytechnic Institution. Martin & Chamberlain designed an Out-Patients' Department in 1869 on the opposite side of Steelhouse Lane, on the corner of Upper Priory. In the following year the original building was vacated and the department transferred to a building in Broad Street that had been used from 1842 to 1868 as a lying-in hospital to provide maternity care for sick women. A new wing was added to the premises in Broad Street in 1875 and alterations were carried out in 1899 by Martin & Chamberlain. In the same year, the practice designed additions to the Steelhouse Lane building.

In 1915 the Children's Hospital moved to new buildings in Ladywood Road, designed by Martin & Martin, where it remained until recently when a move was made back to Steelhouse Lane and the General Hospital building, now named the Diana, Princess of Wales Children's Hospital.

The Orthopaedic and Spinal Hospital had many homes in its early days but settled down when it moved into premises in Great Charles Street, on the corner of Newhall Street, in 1858, and for which Osborn & Reading designed additions in 1888. The hospital, which at some stage became the Royal Orthopaedic Hospital, moved to the premises in Broad Street vacated by the Children's Hospital, and later moved to the Woodlands, Bristol Road, Northfield, where it is still based.

A Homeopathic Hospital was built in Easy Row in 1873, designed by Yeoville Thomason, with extensions by Crouch & Butler in 1898 and 1901. The building was two storeys high, plus an attic, but was significantly higher than its three-storey neighbours. It was four bays wide, each different, with a grotesque entrance in the left inner bay and another entrance in the right outer bay, with an oriel window above it. There were gables to the outer bays and gabled dormer windows to the middle bays, two in the left and a larger one in the right. Not a building to be greatly missed.

The Birmingham and Midland Hospital for Women was opened in the Crescent in 1871. In 1878 the Out-Patients' Department moved to a new building in Upper Priory, designed by Martin & Chamberlain, and the In-Patients' Department moved to Stratford Road, Sparkhill, to the house of Miss Louisa Ann Ryland. A new hospital was built in Showell Green Lane, Sparkhill, in 1906, designed by Martin & Martin, who had designed an extension to the Out-Patients' Department in 1905. I do not know when it moved from Upper Priory. The Women's Hospital is now sited on the University Hospital site in Edgbaston.

The first part of what became **Selly Oak Hospital** was opened in 1877 as King's Norton Union Workhouse in Raddlebarn Road, and was designed by Edward Holmes for the Guardians of the Poor. In later years it was used by the Physiotherapy Department. In 1896 Daniel Arkell designed the Workhouse Infirmary, comprising a central block flanked by two-storey wings at right angles to the road and forming an 'H'. In the same year Arkell made a separate application for a water tower.

The Birmingham and Midland Skin and Urinary Hospital, at 71–9 John Bright Street, was designed by James & Lister Lea, the date on the building indicating that it was built in 1881. It is three storeys high, plus a basement, and four bays wide, each advancing to the road from the left and built in brick with stucco dressings. The left bay has two twin windows at each floor, below two triangular pediments. The second bay houses the entrance and has been extended. The third bay has pairs of narrow windows, a polygonal tower and cupola. The fourth bay, at second-floor level, has a triple window, with a round head over the centre and relief panels at the sides, with shaped sides above leading to a pediment. The building is Grade II listed and is no longer a hospital.

The Lunatic Asylum in Lodge Road was not able to cope with the number of inmates and so an additional asylum was built at Rubery Hill in 1882 at a cost of £132,000, a considerable sum for the time. The premises were designed by Martin & Chamberlain, who were also responsible for extensions in 1890 and 1893. The hospital closed down in the early 1990s and all that remains are the Chapel, the Lodge at 1959 Bristol Road South and the Medical Superintendent's House, all Grade II listed.

The first **Eye Hospital** in Birmingham opened in Cannon Street in 1824, moved later to the former Polytechnic Institution building in Steelhouse Lane and transferred to the Royal Hotel in Temple Row. In 1883 it moved again to a new building on the corner of Church Street and Edmund Street, designed by Payne & Talbot. The building is three storeys high, plus an attic, and is built in red brick, terracotta and stone. The main entrance is in Church Street in a projecting bay, three windows wide and capped with a triangular pediment. The most prominent feature is an oriel window at first-floor level on the angled corner. The building is now occupied by the Hotel du Vin, but the hotel does not offer the medical service so admirably provided by the Royal Hotel those many years ago.

The Scarlet Fever Hospital was built in 4½ acres of land purchased from the Asylum in Lodge Road in the early 1880s, the building work commencing in 1883. In March 1884 two more wards and administrative offices were added, and this was followed by more administrative accommodation and pavilions in 1895. All of the buildings were designed by Martin & Chamberlain. The complex became part of All Saints' Hospital and is now looking for a new use. All Saints' Hospital is Grade II listed.

Jaffray Hospital was built in 1884–5 to the design of Yeoville Thomason, and the building and furnishings were paid for by John Jaffray. It closed down in 1991 and was demolished about four years later. The building was constructed in red brick and terracotta and was two storeys high, with an attic in the central entrance bay. This bay was flanked each side by slightly recessed bays and then there were projecting outer wings, with hipped roofs.

The Ear and Throat Infirmary moved to a new building on the corner of Edmund Street and Barwick Street, designed by Cossins & Peacock, in 1891. An Institution for the Relief of Deafness had been founded by William Dutton in 1844. It started in Cannon Street, moved first to Cherry Street, and then to 45 Ann Street. It amalgamated with the Eye and Ear Dispensary, but as there was already an eye hospital

Eye Hospital, Church Street – now Hotel du Vin. *(Birmingham Central Library)*

Ear and Throat Infirmary, Edmund Street.

this section closed, and the two institutions became the Ear and Throat Infirmary. From Ann Street it moved into the building on the corner of Great Charles Street and Newhall Street, occupied by the Orthopaedic and Spinal Hospital, and from there to the Edmund Street building.

The building is faced in red brick and terracotta and is three storeys high, with a basement and attic. The main part of the frontage to Edmund Street is symmetrical, three bays wide, with a small addition to the right. The two outer bays are advanced, with volutes reducing the width, at first-floor level. There are pairs of windows at each floor and the bays are crowned by Dutch gables. The centre bay has a door at ground floor, with a prominent window above, rising through two floors, divided into three vertical sections and finished with a segmental arch. At roof level there is a dormer window, with a triangular pediment. In the first bay of the return to Barwick Street there is a door opening with a semicircular head, sitting in a wide chimney shaft, which rises through the centre of the Dutch gable.

At some time the name changed to Birmingham Ear and Throat Hospital. The Grade II listed building is being redeveloped and patients are welcome at University Hospital, as far as I know.

An Infections Hospital was built on the Yardley Road, Bordesley Green East, in 1893, following an outbreak of smallpox, and this was the beginning of what is, today, Heartlands Hospital. The hospital was designed by W.H. Ward, who added pavilions and nurses' homes in 1903. The 1893 drawings are not in the archives at Central Library and I do not know what the building looked like and whether it remains. I have seen an illustration dated 1910, showing a two-storey building with a hipped roof, but further research is needed to ascertain what was provided in 1893.

CHAPTER 9

RESIDENTIAL BUILDINGS

During the Victorian period nearly all houses were built privately, the majority for letting, but many for sale. Most developments from the 1870s, when building applications were made or there are, at least, records, were for small numbers of houses, although there were also some comparatively large developments.

Until nearly the end of the nineteenth century the Council was not empowered to build houses, and then only two schemes were carried out. They were close to each other and suffered the same fate, both being demolished in the 1970s to make way for Aston University. The first project was in 1889, when twenty-two houses were designed by Martin & Chamberlain, twenty fronting Ryder Street, between Old Cross Street and Gem Street. The other two were built on the Gem Street return, snuggling up to the rear of the Gaiety Palace. The communal facilities, such as wash-houses and lavatories, were at the other end of the yard, side-on to Old Cross Street. The rent for these houses was 5s 6d a week, too expensive for the poorest classes. The other application was made in 1891 for eighty-one or eight-two houses. The development was sited in Lawrence Street, between Old Cross Street and Duke Street, and the majority of the dwellings were in terraces of eight, built at right angles to Lawrence Street. The architect was A.H. Davis.

The one development that does stand out, and remains, is at Bournville. When Cadbury Brothers moved the factory in 1879, seventeen houses, one detached and sixteen semi-detached, designed by George Gadd, were built to house key employees. However, this had no connection with the development that became the Bournville Estate. The original development plan was produced in 1894 by A.P. Walker, the estate's surveyor, who also designed the first houses. In 1895 W.A. Harvey was appointed architect to the estate at the age of twenty, and he remained in the position until 1904, when he went into private practice, although he continued as consultant to the estate. Although other architects made significant contributions, it is Harvey who is most remembered, not only for his houses but also as the architect of many of the most important buildings, though these were not designed until the twentieth century. I do not know how many houses had been built by the end of Queen Victoria's reign, but it was in the hundreds and the estate was recognised not only nationally but internationally. Several of the houses have been listed. The estate became the Bournville Village Trust in December 1900.

This chapter is devoted, in the main, to individual houses designed for specific clients. In a few instances I have included pairs of houses when I have considered them of note, but there are so many buildings to choose from that very many have been omitted that would otherwise deserve inclusion. Most architects designed houses, but from my research none designed as many as Crouch & Butler.

I know nothing of the biographies of Joseph Crouch and Edmund Butler, although I believe Crouch was born in 1859. Many years ago I read a book written by them, *The Apartments of the House*, from which I assumed that their practice consisted of a small group of select clients with little work, if any, of an industrial or commercial nature. How wrong I was, for the practice carried on a wide range of work and few architects seemed to be as busy. In addition to individual houses, the practice was responsible for several housing schemes involving quite large numbers, and it is also mentioned in the chapters on Corporation Street, Board Schools, Hospitals, Religious Buildings and the Jewellery Quarter. Early in the twentieth century Rupert Savage became a partner, and the firm practises today under the name of Crouch, Butler & Savage.

I shall describe the houses in three groups, Edgbaston, General and Sutton Coldfield, and they will generally be listed in the order they were built. I will keep my descriptions brief, and unless indicated otherwise the buildings are Grade II listed.

EDGBASTON

38 and 39 Frederick Road. I have seen the dates 1848 and 1850 attributed to these houses, designed by J.A. Chatwin, when he worked for Branson & Gwyther, building contractors. As he was not born until 1830, even if the later date is accepted, it is a fine building to be designed by one so young. The houses are faced in stucco, are two storeys high, and each is three bays wide, with the central entrance bay slightly advanced and the openings having semicircular heads.

12 Ampton Road. This house was built in 1855 by J.H. Chamberlain for himself. It is two storeys high, plus attic, and built in red brick, with polychrome brick, tile and stone dressings. The roofs have patterned slates and steep gable ends. I assume he moved from here to Whetstone, at the junction of Farquhar Road and Somerset Road.

50 Carpenter Road. A Martin & Chamberlain house, I understand, of 1870, of red brick, with polychrome brick banding, stone dressings and decorative tile work. It is two storeys high, with attics, and has two gables to the front.

Berrow Court, Berrow Drive. If the practice Martin & Chamberlain was asked to design a house, it was normally in Edgbaston. This house, of 1870–5, was built for Archibald Kenrick, the father of Harriet, the first wife of Joseph Chamberlain. After Harriet's death a few days after the birth of her son Austen, Joseph and his two children moved in with his parents-in-law, but this house was not built until after Joseph's second marriage, to Florence Kenrick, Harriet's cousin. To add a little more interest, Mary, Joseph's sister, married William, Harriet's brother. The house is two storeys high, plus attics, 'L'-shaped in plan and built in red brick, with stone dressings and ornamentation. The steep-pitched, gabled roofs are tiled. It is Grade II* listed. After the Second World War the house was converted into a hotel. It closed in 1988, was refurbished some years later and is once more a hotel.

Knutsford Lodge, 25 Somerset Road. This is a Grade II* listed two-storey building, of 1889, designed by William Henman. It is built in red brick, with stone dressings, in a Jacobean style, with a wealth of shaped gables surrounding the entrance area and oriel windows, with strapwork over.

20 Westfield Road, incorporating 2A Woodbourne Road. Described as a 'Wrenaissance' house, it was designed by J.L. Ball in 1893, and was built in red brick, with thin stone sill courses to both floors. The entrance elevation, to Westfield Road, is three bays wide, with a pediment to the central bay. The return is five bays wide, with rectangular bay windows at ground-floor level.

24 Priory Road. This house, designed by Martin & Chamberlain, was built for J.T. Bunce, the editor of the *Birmingham Post*, in 1893–6, but he did not have long in which to enjoy it, as he died in 1898. It is two storeys high, with an attic floor in the steep gable, and is built in red brick, with stone dressings. There is an oriel bow window to the entrance front and two square bay oriels to the garden front, but don't go to admire the garden, for the house is part of Priory Hospital.

17 and 19 Rotton Park Road. A pair of semi-detached houses of 1896, designed by J.L. Ball, who lived at no. 17. The houses are built in brick, are two storeys high, plus attic, and each house is three bays wide. There is a gabled porch in the centre bay of each house, canted bay windows in the two centre bays and gabled dormer windows in the four inner bays.

The Homestead, 25 Woodbourne Road. This is one of the most important houses in Birmingham, designed by Bateman & Bateman in the Arts and Crafts style in 1897, and Grade I listed. The house is 'L'-shaped, double pile, with the main front facing south, to the garden, and the entrance in the west front of the rear wing. The house is two storeys high, with an attic to the west end of the garden front. The finish is primarily roughcast, and the roofs have stone slates.

21 Yateley Road. It is fortuitous that the only other Grade I listed Victorian house in Birmingham should be next to its companion in this very select group. The architect H.T. Buckland designed it for his own occupation in 1899 and he lived there until his death in 1951. I believe that in both houses an important factor in their listing was the virtually unaltered state of the interiors. This Arts and Crafts house has a pebble-dashed exterior and tiled roof. It is two storeys high, with an attic in the gable, rising above eaves level over the entrance porch, which has a semicircular hood. There is a canted bay window at ground-floor level, to the left of the entrance, and the other windows are casements, placed and sized as needed.

Garth House, 47 Edgbaston Park Road.

Buckland & Haywood-Farmer designed, also, 13, 15, 17 and 19 Yateley Road and William Henman designed no. 11 and another house for himself, but I do not know which.

Garth House, 47 Edgbaston Park Road. A Grade II* listed house of 1901, by W.H. Bidlake, one of Birmingham's finest architects. It is based on an 'L' plan of irregular shape, with a four-storey, square, brick tower at the internal angle. The remainder of the house is built of red brick, at ground-floor level, but the majority of the first floor and above has a roughcast finish. Adjacent to the entrance is a gable, with its only window being to the attic.

GENERAL

Highbury, Yew Tree Road, Moseley. Probably the most famous and the largest of all the houses I shall mention, its fame resting to a considerable extent on the identity of its owner, Joseph Chamberlain, Birmingham's most famous London-born son. The architect was Martin & Chamberlain, in 1879, and it is Grade II* listed. The facing material is red brick, with stone dressings, and timber work to some of the many gables. The building is two and three storeys high, with many features, including three groups of different bay windows to the garden front and an oriel bow window to the north end of the east elevation. The house has had many uses since Chamberlain's death in 1914, following

Highbury, Yew Tree Road, Moseley.

4 and 6 Stanley Road, King's Heath. *(Birmingham Central Library*

59 Salisbury Road, Moseley. *(Birmingham Central Library*

which his wife and daughters moved away from Birmingham. It is now in the ownership of Birmingham City Council and used as a conference and banqueting centre. This allows an opportunity to see the interior, including the main hall where dinners are held. I arranged one a few years ago and it was a memorable evening.

4 and 6 Stanley Road, King's Heath. A pair of half-timbered Arts and Crafts houses, of 1894–5, designed by Bateman & Bateman. There are a total of six bays, with the ground floor in brick, on a roughcast plinth, and a close-studded first floor. The end bays are slightly lower and gabled. The two central bays are recessed at ground floor, with two small, canted bay windows. The entrances are in the centre bay of each house. (See also 254 Vicarage Road, 2 Cartland Road, 258 Vicarage Road and 1 Cartland Road, also by Bateman & Bateman.)

59 Salisbury Road, Moseley. A two-storey house, designed by Crouch & Butler in 1897, in four bays. The left bay has a canted bay window, with hipped roof, at ground-floor level. The next bay has a recessed entrance and rises above eaves level as a tower, with decorative stone banding at the top. The next bay projects, with bevelled corners and hipped roof, and is half-timbered, with close timber studs from ground-floor window-head level upwards. The right, wider bay has projecting half-timbering from above first-floor level. The main material is brick, with stone dressings.

The Anchorage, 137 Handsworth Wood Road. A Grade II* listed building of 1899, designed by Crouch & Butler in the Arts and Crafts style. The finishes are brick, with stone dressings, with some applied timber framing to the right side, and tile roofs. A cupola is placed asymmetrically between brick gable and lower half-timber bay, incorporating the porch.

18 Dora Road, Small Heath, was built as a vicarage for St Oswald's Church in 1899, and was designed by the architect of the church, W.H. Bidlake. It is a two-storey building in red facing bricks, with hipped, tile roofs. A wing projects at the right, with a large canted bay window at ground-floor level. The property is now known as St Oswald's Court.

5 and 6 Holly Grove, Bournville is small sample of the work of W.A. Harvey from 1900. The building is a pair of semi-detached houses, symmetrical in layout, two storeys high and four bays wide. The two inner bays are advanced, with separate gables. The ground floor is of brick, with slate tile hanging above. The entrances are in the outer bays and there are canted bay windows in the inner bays. At first-floor level there are rectangular bay windows, on brackets, to the inner bays. (See also 1–4, 7–10, and 11 and 12 Holly Grove, and many more.)

100 Sampson Road, Sparkbrook. This fine Grade II* listed building was designed by W.H. Bidlake in 1901 as the vicarage of St Agatha's Church. It is a large, irregular-shaped, brick, two-storey dwelling, with an almost blank south elevation looking onto Claremont Road. The elevation to Sampson Road is attractive, with an oriel above the entrance and a canted bay window to the right.

100 Sampson Road, Sparkbrook.

SUTTON COLDFIELD

The Four Oaks Estate in Sutton Coldfield probably had more Arts and Crafts houses built on it than any other comparable area within the present-day boundaries of Birmingham. One reason for this may have been that development of the estate began in the 1890s. A good proportion of the houses remain, although the most important one, The Hurst, in Hartopp Road, one of only six major buildings designed by W.R. Lethaby (see 122 and 124 Colmore Row), was one of the first to be demolished. I shall finish by noting a few of these houses, but other areas also had fine dwellings. Beginning at the top of Digby Road, I shall go around the corner into the Driffold, where Crouch & Butler designed six houses, including those for themselves.

Seven Gables, 14 Digby Road. This house, on the corner of Digby Road and the Driffold, was built in 1898 by Joseph Crouch for his own occupation. It is mainly a two-storey house, rising to two and a half storeys above the hall, which is one and a half storeys high. The main facing material is red brick, with half timbering above ground floor to the hall section and the left end of the north elevation and the return onto the east elevation. There are canted bay windows at ground floor on the south elevation, a bow window to the hall, and a canted bay window to the first-floor landing. There are interesting tower-like structures to the north and south sides and, by my counting, seven gables.

Top o' the Hill, 14 Driffold. Not to be outdone, a year later Edmund Butler built his own house in the Driffold, just down from the other side of Digby Road. The entrance to the site was through a wrought-iron gate directly opposite the left side of the house, which had a stepped gable leading to a chimney stack, a popular detail with Crouch & Butler. The original entrance to the house has been obscured by a single-storey addition containing a new entrance. To the right there is a projecting wing with bevelled corners, hipped roof and half timbering, similar to 59 Salisbury Road. Beyond that, to the right, is a half-timbered gable. Walls are rendered from about 3ft high, with brickwork under, all painted white. The building is not listed.

Wyndhurst, 12 Driffold. This house, next door to Top o' the Hill, is two storeys high, plus an attic, and the main feature of the front is two contrasting gables. The one to the left is half-timbered from the first floor upwards and the one to the right is brick and is splayed, with a window wrapping round it at first-floor level and a sundial, in stone, over. On the left return there is a stepped gable, culminating in a chimney, as next door. It is not listed. (See also, by Crouch & Butler, The Homestead, 11 Digby Road, of 1897, Grade II listed, and 7 and 9 Driffold, of 1890–4.)

The Leasowes, 107 Lichfield Road, was designed in 1893 by Ernest Newton, a nationally known architect and Lethaby's predecessor as chief assistant to Norman Shaw. The house is two storeys high, plus attics. The front is divided into three main sections, all prominent. At the left there is a large, two-storey bow window and then a projecting, battlemented and domed tower, housing a round-headed entrance porch.

At the right there are twin gables, with white-painted weather boarding. Under this there is half-timbering down to first-floor level, although I believe this has replaced tile hanging, There is a plentiful supply of bay windows of different designs. The main facing material is brick.

Withens, 17 Barker Road, Four Oaks. Barker Road is to the side of the Four Oaks Estate, with houses of quality. This one was designed by W.H. Bidlake in 1899 and is two storeys high, plus attic, and five bays wide, the outer ones projecting, with gables. The left bay is unpierced and the right one has a large canted bay window to the ground floor and a Venetian type window above. The centre bay comprises a two-storey porch entrance, with stone surround and stone and brick quoins. Above the entrance there is a canted bay oriel. The window frame to the oriel is stone and the remaining windows are of wood. The main facing material is brick.

32 Barker Road, Four Oaks. The entrance to this two-storey, plus attic, house, designed by Cossins, Peacock & Bewlay in 1901, is on the elevation at right angles to the road, but it is the road elevation I will describe. The road front is three bays wide and the main facing material is brick. The centre bay is gabled and projects slightly, with a shallow canted bay window at first floor and a Venetian type window in the gable. The right, entrance front return has a two-storey bay, with tile hanging between the windows and, in the gable, a window to match the one on the road front.

From here we move on to the Four Oaks Estate. I shall mention very few houses in any detail and will only refer to others, but many important houses were built in the early years of the twentieth century and so are not included here, other than some receiving a brief mention. I shall start at the lower end of Hartopp Road, the first road to be developed, by the Hartopp gate entrance to Sutton Park, and with a very important dwelling:

Woodgate, 37 Hartopp Road, was built by W.H. Bidlake for his own occupation. It is on the corner of Ladywood Road and is tucked well into the original site. It is two storeys high, plus attics, and the south (garden) front has two gabled projections, each with a bay window at ground floor and a three-light window to the first floor. Between the projections there is a door opening to the garden. The tiled roof, to the rest of the elevation, sweeps down to first-floor window-sill level. Around the corner, on

32 Barker Road, Four Oaks.

the west front, there is a canted, single-storey projection with a hipped roof. The main facing material is brick.

Oakwood, 34 Hartopp Road. This building was originally the lodge to The Hurst, referred to in the preamble to Sutton Coldfield, and was built in the period 1897–1901, designed by Lethaby & Ball. The building has been altered and extended and so is not referred to in detail.

Luttrell House, 18 Hartopp Road. One reason for selecting this house is that it was designed by E.F. Titley, who designed many more houses on Four Oaks Estate than any other architect and lived at Beechwood, 12 Hartopp Road, now demolished. Luttrell House was built in 1898 and is two storeys high and, to the road, is three bays wide.

The ground floor is brick with stone dressings, and above is half-timbered. The outer bays are gabled and the left bay has, at ground floor, a canted bay window in a stone surround. The entrance porch is in the slightly recessed middle bay and is brought forward to marry up with the brickwork of the left bay and has a round-headed entrance door set in a stone surround. The house is not listed.

Continue along Hartopp Road passing Briarwood at no. 6, on the left, an unlisted house, designed by Cossins & Peacock in 1896, and Redlands, at no. 1, designed by Bateman & Bateman in 1893, with extensions built in 1903.

Woodside, 51 Bracebridge Road, Four Oaks.

Turn right into Four Oaks Road and, on the corner of Luttrell Road, observe no. 21, Avoncroft, designed by Crouch & Butler in 1899, and then turn right into Luttrell Road.

As you walk along Luttrell Road you will have to exercise considerable restraint to ignore Carhampton House, on the left, at no. 11, as Bateman & Bateman did not design it until 1902. You must be even firmer when you pass nos 16 and 18, for Crouch & Butler waited until 1907 and 1906 before designing these houses.

Do not think that things will get much better after you have turned left into Bracebridge Road, for you will be tempted by two houses on the left, designed by architects for their own occupation, but almost certainly not begun until 1902 and 1904 respectively. Hawkesford, at no. 14, was designed by C.E. Bateman for his father and himself, and their next-door neighbour, at The Grange, no. 12, was E. Hayward-Farmer, of Buckland & Hayward-Farmer.

On the opposite side of the road is Woodside, no. 51, designed by W.H. Bidlake in 1897, but now much enlarged. A little further down, on the same side and on the near corner, is Yates House, at 22 Ladywood Road, also designed by Bidlake but not until 1902.

Further down Bracebridge Road and on the same side is Bryn Teg, no. 35, once again designed out of time, in 1904, by Bateman & Bateman. I will conclude with a brief description of a house on the opposite side of the road and then leave you to find your way home. Four Oaks railway station is nearby.

The Dene, 2 Bracebridge Road was the first house designed by W.H. Bidlake, in 1895–6, and is two storeys high, plus an attic. At the left, looking from the road, there is tile hanging down to the ground-floor window heads, with a small, shallow canted bay window, supported on brackets, at ground floor at the left end. Around the corner, at the left end, there is a deep, single-storey bay window with a hipped roof. The tile hanging is ended at the right by a two-storey tower which contains the entrance door. Beyond that, and projecting from the tower, is a gabled wing with half-timbering down to the ground-floor window heads and bracketed out proud of the brickwork below.

The Dene, 2 Bracebridge Road, Four Oaks.

OTHER RESIDENTIAL BUILDINGS

This section is confined almost exclusively to almshouses, with a mention of one orphanage.

The best-known and longest-lasting almshouses in Birmingham are those provided by Lench's Trust, set up as a charity by William Lench in 1525. The first almshouse was built in Digbeth in the early seventeenth century, and the biggest was erected in Steelhouse Lane, between nos 88 and 95 on land later to be occupied by the General Hospital, in 1764; it was demolished in the 1880s.

According to the telephone directory, Lench's Trust still operates at the following addresses, whether they are all almshouses I do not know: 271 Hagley Road; 118 Conybere Street; 231 Ladywood Middleway; Lench's Close, Wake Green Road; 80 Ridgeacre Road and 128 Whitehouse Common Road, Sutton Coldfield. There is the significant omission of Ravenhurst Street, which suggests that there may be more. The buildings on three sites are Grade II listed and worthy of description.

Ravenhurst Street, Highgate. These almshouses were built in 1849 and designed by Hornblower & Haylock. The facing materials were red brick and stone dressings. The elevation to the street is symmetrical, centred on the Matron's lodge, with flanking walls to each side connecting to the gable ends of wings stretching back to form a close. The lodge is two storeys high, with an attic and ogee-shaped gable and, facing the close, there is a two-storey canted bay window, with a three-light attic casement above, surmounted by a shaped gable. The two-storey wings are divided into three-bay sections facing the close, each containing three almshouses. The far end is closed by a pair of almshouses, with a break in the centre.

Ladywood Road (231 Ladywood Middleway). Hornblower was able to combine his naval career with his architectural practice. Nine years after designing Ravenhurst Street, Hornblower & Haylock was asked to build another block in Ladywood Road and decided there could be no improvement on facing bricks and stone dressings for the facing materials. There is also a familiar look to the two-storey matron's lodge in the centre and the gabled wings, but it seems to be a sensible arrangement. The lodge has a tripartite, mullioned and transomed window at ground-floor level and a tripartite mullioned window above, followed by a shaped gable. The gables to the wings have decorated tripartite panels to the front and each wing contains six almshouses, with porches rising through two storeys, each giving entry to three. The lodge has a two-storey canted bay window on the inner face. The building is in the Jacobean style.

118 Conybere Street, Highgate. J.A. Chatwin was the architect for this project, carried out in 1879. The development comprised a close of two-storey, red-brick almshouses built along three sides of a rectangular green, with a warden's house in the centre of the open end to the street. The elevations to the green are simple, with gables breaking up the line of the eaves. The elevations to the road are more decorative, with hipped roofs to the buildings and an elaborate, slightly advanced centre feature topped with a gable. At ground- and first-floor levels to the outer houses

Almshouses, Ravenhurst Street.

there are coupled windows, with a brick, triangular feature above each upper window, embracing a circular attic window set in a (almost) diamond setting. At ground-floor level of the warden's house an inscribed plaque is substituted for the windows. The buildings were linked to each other by a tall screen wall consisting of large, round-headed openings between piers. The tall ribbed chimneys are another feature.

Rhodes' Almshouses, 80–6 Soho Road, Handsworth. I know very little about this charity or its mid-nineteenth-century Jacobean-style building. It is a two-storey, three-bay building, of brick with stone dressings. The outer bays are advanced, with broad, shaped gables and the inner bay has little ogee gables separated by the doors. Windows are two-light casements, except for canted bay windows to the ground floor of the outer bays.

The Quadrangle, Maryvale Road, Bournville. These attractive almshouses were designed by Ewen Harper in 1897 for Richard Cadbury, and are controlled by the Bournville Almshouse Trust. They are built in red brick, with stone dressings, in a Tudor style, and are single storey, sited around a spacious quadrangle. The buildings are symmetrically arranged to the front, with a central, two-storey gatehouse, with a projecting porch, an oriel window over, and a shaped gable flanked by turrets. There is a single-storey wing each side of the gatehouse, the one to the left for the matron and that to the right for a chapel. The almshouses have canted bay windows to the road and they and the wings have central and end gables. In the quadrangle there are

Almshouses, Conybere Street.

round-headed entrances, in pairs, with gables over. In the centre of the quadrangle there is a rectangular shelter, supported on timber columns, with a pyramidal, tiled roof, gabled dormers on all sides and a lantern.

Erdington Cottage Homes is the only Birmingham orphanage that I shall mention here. It is on a site bounded by Fentham Road, The Gardens, Highcroft Road and Reservoir Road. I have a soft spot for the place, as I played a few games of football against the Erdington boys before the Second World War. At the time I took more notice of the football pitch than the buildings.

As it is adjacent to Highcroft Hospital, I assume that the Cottage Homes is an offshoot, and took the children who previously went to the Aston Union Workhouse, but must reiterate that this is an assumption and not the result of research.

The orphanage was built in 1898 and was designed by Franklin, Cross & Nicholas. On each side of a central avenue there are two-storey cottages, alternately detached and semi-detached, with small, canted bay windows to the ground floor. Separate buildings accommodated the chapel and hall (now a leisure centre) and the school. At the midpoint of the avenue there is a tower supported on a timber-frame structure, housing a clock, which is protected by a pyramidal roof.

CHAPTER 10

RELIGIOUS BUILDINGS

During the Victorian period a large number of churches and chapels were built. The following figures (taken from *The Making of Victorian Birmingham* by Victor Skipp) show the growth in the middle part of the century:

	Anglican churches	Nonconformist chapels
1830	12	21
1851	25	54
1872	46	90

In 1835 there were two Roman Catholic churches in Birmingham and this had increased to eight by 1874, with others in Handsworth, Erdington, Oscott and Sutton Coldfield. Despite the smaller number of places of worship, 50 per cent of churchgoers attended Anglican services.

Church and chapel building continued unabated in the last third of the nineteenth century and into the early years of the twentieth century. In addition, a significant number of existing churches were largely rebuilt or extended.

It is not practicable to list all, or even most, of these buildings and I will confine myself to some of the most important of those that still remain, and mention significant earlier churches that were substantially rebuilt. I shall start by discussing an architect who designed far more churches than any other, and who carried out extensions and alterations to many of the more remarkable churches in Birmingham.

J.A. CHATWIN

The architect who designed the most new churches and carried out most alterations to existing churches was Julius Alfred Chatwin (1830–1907). He was born in Great Charles Street and was educated at King Edward's School, New Street. He commenced his architectural career with Branson & Gwyther, building contractors, and while with them designed 38 and 39 Frederick Road, Edgbaston, in 1848, now Grade II listed, and Bingley Hall in 1850, now demolished.

Chatwin went to London and became a pupil of Sir Charles Barry, the architect of King Edward's School, in 1851, and assisted on drawings for the House of Lords. He attended evening classes of the first Schools of Design, originated by Prince Albert and held at the old Royal Academy rooms at Somerset House. Chatwin returned to Birmingham and commenced practice on his own account on 10 October 1855, in

Bennett's Hill, moving from there to 20 Temple Street in December 1858, and then to 128 Colmore Row in 1900.

He married in October 1869 and left four sons and four daughters when he died at his home at 57 Wellington Road, Edgbaston, on 6 June 1907. His son Philip had been in partnership with him for about ten years and continued the practice, being joined later by his nephew, Anthony Chatwin. Philip died in 1964, when the practice, under the title of J.A. Chatwin & Son, was still in existence, under the control of Anthony.

Chatwin had a long and distinguished career, and although he is remembered primarily for his ecclesiastical work he produced many other buildings as well. He designed many buildings in the city centre, of which only one, the earliest, remains. Rather surprisingly, he does not seem to have received any commissions to design civic buildings. An important client was Lloyds Bank, for whom he designed numerous branches, including the local head office in Colmore Row and another in Lombard Street, London. However, this chapter is concerned with his religious buildings, which are listed below.

New churches designed by Chatwin include the following, some of which I shall refer to in a little more detail in the section on Churches and Chapels:

1859–60: St Clement's, Nechells Park Road, Duddeston.
1864: Holy Trinity, Birchfield Road/Trinity Road. Grade II* listed.
1868: St Laurence's, Dartmouth Street. Closed 1951.
1868–76: St Augustine's, Lyttleton Road, Edgbaston. Grade II* listed.
1869: St Gabriel's, Pickford Street/Barn Street. Badly damaged in the Second World War. Closed 1945.
1873: Catholic Apostolic church, Summer Hill. Extended 1900. Now Greek Orthodox church. Grade II listed.
1874: St Saviour's, Villa Street, Lozells. Closed.
1880: St Paul's, Lozells Road. Grade II listed.
1883–5: Christchurch, Summerfield Crescent. Grade II listed.
1888: St Mary's, Bearwood Road.
1890–1: St James's, Frederick Road, Aston. Demolished and replaced.
1894–5: St James's, Crockett Road, Handsworth. New church built at side of existing one.
1897–8: All Saints's, Albert Road, Stechford.
1897–8: St Mary and St Ambrose's, Pershore Road. Grade II listed.
1899: St Mark's, Washwood Heath Road.

Chatwin was involved in substantial rebuilding or extension projects for many churches, including the following important ones:

1872–85: St Martin's, Bull Ring. Main body of church rebuilt. Grade II* listed.
1876–80: St Mary's, Hamstead Road, Handsworth. Extensive rebuilding. Grade II* listed.
1879–90: St Peter and St Paul's, Aston. Extensive rebuilding. Grade II* listed. This is

St Martin's, Bull Ring.

the only church within the boundaries of Birmingham to have been mentioned in the Domesday Survey.

1883: St Philip's, Colmore Row (cathedral). Chancel extended. Grade I listed.

1884–5: St George's, Westbourne Crescent, Edgbaston. New nave and chancel. Grade II listed.

1885: St Bartholomew's, Church Road, Edgbaston. Chancel, chapels and north arcade added and, in 1889, a second south aisle. Grade II listed.

1886: St Mary's, St Mary's Row, Moseley. North aisle added and, in 1897, chapel extended and side chapel added. Grade II listed.

Among the records in the Central Reference Library the following church schools are attributed to J.A. Chatwin. I am sceptical of the date 1839 for St Matthew's, as J.A. Chatwin was not born until 1830. It is interesting to note that these schools were all built before the Elementary Education Act of 1870 and the advent of Board schools.

1839/59/79: St Matthew's School, Lupin Street, Duddeston. Lupin Street no longer exists.

1851: St Silas's National School, Church Street, Lozells.

1858–68: St Clement's National School, High Park Street, Nechells.

1861: St Anne's National School, Devon Street, Duddeston.

1867: St Laurence's National School, Dartmouth Street. Demolished.

1867: St Mary's Church School, Whitehouse Street/Avenue Road, Aston.

1868: Bishop Ryder School, Staniforth Street.

CHURCH OF ENGLAND

Unless stated otherwise, all churches described here were built in the Gothic style.

St George's, Westbourne Crescent/Westbourne Road. The original church of 1836–8 consisted of nave and aisles in an Early English style, designed by J.J. Scoles and, to this, a chancel was added in 1856 by Charles Edge. A photograph taken in 1873 shows an attractive church. A new nave and chancel were built in 1884–5, designed by J.A. Chatwin. The building is of sandstone and is Grade II listed.

St John's, Walmley Road.

St John's, Walmley Road, Sutton Coldfield. This church was built in 1845 and the architect was D.R. Hill, who did not live long enough to see Nikolaus Pevsner describe it as 'a fascinating horror'. It is a Norman-style building, built in blue bricks, with a west rose window and bellcote and is Grade II listed. I can see what Pevsner meant, but would rather emphasise the 'fascinating' than the 'horror'.

St Saviour's, St Saviour's Road, Saltley. A large Perpendicular-style church in red and yellow sandstone, consecrated in 1850. The architect was R.C. Hussey and the building is Grade II listed. The building comprises aisled and clerestoried nave of four bays with six-light windows, chancel, transepts with five-light windows, north porch and south tower with prominent stair turret. A spire was added to the tower in 1871, but was removed later.

St John's, Monument Road/Wood Street, Ladywood. This was built in 1852–4 to the design of S.S. Teulon, and comprised nave, chancel and tower. Chancel aisles and transepts were added in 1884–5 by J.A. Chatwin. The building is of stone, in the Decorated style, and Grade II listed. Recently the interior has been imaginatively remodelled.

St Silas's, Church Street, Lozells was built in 1854, the architect was F.W. Fiddian and it is Grade II listed. It is built of brick, with a slate roof, has lancet windows and is cruciform in plan, comprising chancel, nave and transepts.

St Michael's, St Michael's Road, Handsworth, 1855, was designed by W. Bourne and comprised chancel, nave, aisles, transepts and tower, to which a spire was added in 1868. The facing material is sandstone and it is a Grade II listed building. This is the church in which I was baptised.

St Mary's, Bristol Road, Selly Oak. Edward Holmes was the architect of this Grade II listed building of 1861. It is built in the Decorated style, with two colour tones of sandstone giving a banded appearance, and the steep nave roof has bands of tiles. There is a chancel, nave, transepts and north-west tower, with a broached spire. I was married in this church.

St Michael's, Handsworth.

St Augustine's, Edgbaston.

Holy Trinity, Trinity Road, Birchfield. Built in 1864, to the design of J.A. Chatwin, and Grade II* listed. There is a chancel, nave, aisles and south-west tower and spire. It is faced with red stone, with sandstone dressings.

St Peter's, Old Church Road, Harborne. This church was rebuilt in 1867 – except for the fifteenth-century tower – in red sandstone, to match the tower. The rebuilding comprised nave, aisles, transepts with galleries and an apsidal chancel. The architect was Yeoville Thomason and the building is Grade II listed.

Christ Church, Grantham Road, Sparkbrook was designed by Medland, Maberley & Medland in 1867, was faced in brick and stone. The accommodation comprised a two-bay buttressed chancel, nave with decorative tile roof, aisles with six gables and south-west tower with a spire, which was taken down after suffering blast damage in the Second World War. The church is to be demolished after being badly damaged in the tornado of July 2005.

St Augustine's, Lyttleton Road, Edgbaston. A church of 1868, Grade II* listed and designed by J.A. Chatwin, dominated by the tower and spire added in 1876. The original building, faced with sandstone, with limestone banding and a tiled roof, comprised a polygonal buttressed chancel, nave, aisles, transepts and porch.

St Stephen's, Serpentine Road, Selly Oak. A Grade II listed building, designed in 1870 by Martin & Chamberlain (but not easily recognised as the work of that practice), in a Decorated style, comprising apsidal chancel, steeply pitched tall nave with decorative tile roof and south-west tower, with a broached spire.

St Cyprian with St Chad's, The Fordrough, Hay Mills. From a church not easily recognisable as by Martin & Chamberlain to one that is, although it is actually by F.B. Osborn. I went to see it thinking that it was by Martin & Chamberlain and came away with my belief unshaken. It was only when I read Osborn's obituary that I discovered that he had designed it. The church is built in red brick, with small amounts of blue brick and stone dressings, and has tiled roofs. It comprises a chancel, nave, low narrow aisles demarcated by buttresses and single lancet windows, the Horsfall mortuary chapel to the south-east and a south-west tower, accommodating the entrance and

St Anne's, Moseley.

St Alban the Martyr's, Bordesley.

with a broached spire. The church was provided by James Horsfall and built next door to his factory, and is approached from an island where the Small Heath Highway joins the Coventry Road, at its east end. It was built in 1873–4 and is Grade II listed.

St Anne's, Park Hill, Moseley. A stone building of 1874, designed by F. Preedy, and Grade II listed. The church has a tall, clerestoried nave, low aisles, short chancel, projecting, polygonal west baptistery and tall north-west tower, with pinnacles and spire.

St Alban the Martyr's, Conybere Street, Bordesley. This is one of the most important churches built in Birmingham during the Victorian period. It is of 1879–81, designed by J.L. Pearson, an architect of national repute, and is Grade II* listed. The church was designed in the Early English style, with a cruciform plan, and faced with red brick, with stone dressings and some diaper work. There is an apsidal chancel, clerestoried nave aisles, transepts and north and south chapels. The south-west tower was not added until 1938, by E.F. Reynolds. I have, in all cases, concentrated on the exterior of the buildings, but this one you should enter, for it is recognised that the interior is its main glory.

St Paul's, Lozells Road, Lozells, of 1880, was designed by J.A. Chatwin and is Grade II listed. The west front, to the road, is faced in stone and the remainder is brick. The church comprises nave, aisles, apsidal chancel and north-west tower, all in a Perpendicular style.

Christ Church, Summerfield Crescent, Winson Green, designed by J.A. Chatwin, in 1883–5, in a Perpendicular style and Grade II listed. The building, faced in stone, has clerestoried nave, aisles, transepts and apsidal chancel.

St Agnes's, Colmore Crescent, Moseley. A Grade II listed building in the Decorated style, built in sandstone, with chancel, nave, low buttressed aisles and short transepts. There is also a tower, which was in a truncated form with a shallow pyramidal roof until its completion in 1932. The church was consecrated in 1884 and enlarged in 1893, but I do not know which parts date from each period. The architect was William Davis, whose design won in competition.

St John the Evangelist's, Stratford Road and St John's Road. A Grade II listed church, of 1889, by Martin & Chamberlain, faced in red brick, with terracotta and stone, and built in an Early English style. The church comprises nave, transepts, chancel, vestry and tower, to which a spire was added in 1905. It is a strong, spare church, with a profusion of gables and an unusual interior.

St Paul's, Walsall Road, Hamstead. William Davis was the architect of this church, of 1892, which built in the Decorated style in brick and stone, with nave, aisles, transepts and octagonal chancel.

St Agnes's, Moseley.

St Oswald's, St Oswald's Road, Small Heath. This was the first of an outstanding group of church buildings designed by W.H. Bidlake and was designed in 1892, with the west front added in 1899, and is Grade II* listed. The original building, constructed in red brick, with stone dressings and a tiled roof, is a simple, lofty building with lancet windows, but the later west front is much more elaborate, in the Decorated style. The church contained chancel, tall clerestoried nave, aisles, transepts and west-facing porches. It is no longer used as a church and when I was there a sign on the front proclaimed it as 'Hamid House Preparatory School'.

St Aidan's, Herbert Road, Small Heath. This is another Grade II* listed building, designed by Thomas Proud, built in 1893–8 in the Perpendicular style, of red brick, with buff terracotta dressings. The nave and chancel are all in one and there are also narrow, windowless aisles, chapel and west apsidal baptistery.

Chapels, Brandwood End Cemetery, Woodthorpe Road, King's Heath. This Grade II listed building, of 1897, consists of a central entrance, with a squat tower and spire over, flanked on both sides by a chapel, one Church of England and the other Nonconformist, each having elaborate gabled, buttressed and pinnacled fronts. The architect was J. Brewin Holmes, who I believe may be the son of Edward Holmes.

St Mary and St Ambrose's, Pershore Road, Edgbaston. This is another church by J.A. Chatwin, built in 1897–8, and Grade II listed. The building occupies an open position on the left side of Pershore Road going from the city centre, is faced in red brick and red terracotta, and comprises chancel with aisle, nave, aisles, vestries, south-west apsidal baptistery and north-west tower and spire. Its siting gives prominence to the tower and baptistery.

St Agatha's, Stratford Road, Sparkbrook. I am very pleased to finish the group with the only Grade I listed Victorian church in Birmingham, designed by W.H. Bidlake, the

St Mary and St Ambrose's, Edgbaston.

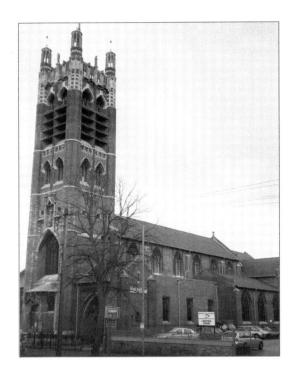

St Agatha's, Sparkbrook.

only architect to have designed three Grade I listed buildings in Birmingham. The building, of 1899–1901, is faced in brick and stone and is dominated by its magnificent, beautifully detailed tower. The building comprises chancel, chapels, nave, aisles, entrance porches each side of the tower and, projecting from a recess in the road front of the tower, a three-sided baptistery. Besides the tower, the other glory of this church is its interior. To see the church is incentive enough, but next to it is one of the very best Board schools, Ladypool School, and almost opposite is Stratford Road Baptist Chapel.

ROMAN CATHOLIC

Cathedral of St Chad, St Chad's Circus, Queensway. I do believe that this building was originally built as a church. It was erected in 1839–41, is Grade II* listed and was designed by A.W.N. Pugin, the most passionate advocate of Gothic architecture in the country. He had been involved with the design of the Houses of Parliament, for which the Gothic style had been insisted on, as it was looked on as an 'English style', and so it is interesting that this building shows that Gothic and Englishness are not necessarily synonymous. This austere, red-brick building, with twin west towers and spires, is more typical of north German architecture. It is an impressive, rather than lovely, building, but is an important feature of Birmingham's architectural scene.

Convent of Our Lady of Mercy, Hunter's Road, Lozells. This Grade II* listed building was constructed in 1840–1 and the architect was A.W.N. Pugin. The materials are red brick, with stone dressings and some diapering, and the steep-pitched roofs of slate have stone copings to the gables with finials. The main range of the 'E'-shaped plan faces the road. The chapel was destroyed during the Second World War and a new chapel was built in the late 1950s.

St Thomas and St Edmund's, Sutton Road, Erdington was built in 1848–50, to the design of Charles Hansom, and is Grade II listed. It is a large, elaborate church in red sandstone, comprising nave, aisles in the form of double aisles, transepts, chancel, four-stage north-west tower, with broached spire and small, vaulted oratory at the south-west corner.

Cathedral of St Chad.

St Thomas and St Edmund's, Erdington.

St Joseph's, Thimblemill Lane and Long Acre, Nechells. This was built originally as a mortuary chapel, with a chancel and north chapel, divided by two wide arches, by A.W.N. Pugin, in 1850. His son, E.W. Pugin, added a five-bay nave and north aisle in 1872. The west front is built in brick, with stone dressings, and is gabled, and there is a porch, with a bell opening above. The building is Grade II listed.

St Mary's, Vivian Road, Harborne. A church of 1877 by Dunn & Hansom, faced with red brick and stone dressings. It comprises a three-bay nave, south aisle, transept, chancel, and an octagonal bell turret at the south-west corner.

St Anne's, Alcester Street, Digbeth, was built in 1884 to the design of Vicars & O'Neill and is constructed in red brick, with bands of darker brick and stone dressings. The nave is separated from wide aisles by Gothic arcades, with lancet windows at clerestory level and in the aisles and a rose window in the chancel. A square north-west tower has an octagonal belfry and short stone spire.

St Francis's, Hunter's Road, Handsworth. I was born in this road and felt rather offended when Pevsner described the church as 'in red brick, with stone dressings in a skimped E.E. style'. It was designed by Canon Scoles in 1894, and has a nave, six bays long, with aisles, a rectangular chancel, north chapel and octagonal north-west baptistery. Skimped indeed.

St Joseph's, Nechells.

St Patrick's, Winson Green.

St Patrick's, Dudley Road, Winson Green. I think I may have been a little harsh on Dempster & Heaton in connection with some of the buildings the practice designed in Corporation Street, for I felt it was capable of better things, as is shown in this church of 1895 and Grade II listed. The facing materials are red brick and stone dressings, and it comprises a nave, aisles, chancel, north-west baptistery and south-west octagonal bell turret. There are two rose windows in the west front.

St John's, George Street, Balsall Heath. This church was built in 1896, in a Romanesque style, and the architect was A. Vicars. There is a nave, aisles, chancel, and bell turret at the south-west corner.

GREEK ORTHODOX

Greek Orthodox Cathedral, Summer Hill Terrace, Ladywood. This was built as the Catholic Apostolic church in 1873, the architect was J.A. Chatwin and it is looked upon as one of his better buildings. It is constructed in red brick and terracotta and is Grade II listed.

NONCONFORMIST

The following is a small selection of the many Nonconformist churches and chapels.

Christ Church Baptist Church, Six Ways, Aston. The church is situated in a prominent position, on a corner site, and the dominant feature is the square tower at the front of the site, surmounted by an octagonal stone spire, flanked by tabernacles at the corners. The building is in a Venetian Gothic style, in polychromatic brick, with stone dressings, and steep-pitched slate roofs. The tower is linked, by a lower entrance bay, to the main church. The building was erected in 1862–5 and the architect was James Cranston of Oxford. It is deservedly Grade II listed. A hall was added in 1888, designed by J.C. Dunn and J.F. Hipkiss.

Methodist Church, South Street, Harborne. I have seen the design of this Grade II listed church, of 1868, attributed to Martin & Chamberlain and have no reason to question this. It is built in red brick with polychrome and stone dressings and has slate

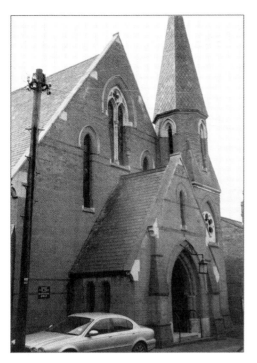

Methodist church, South Street, Harborne.

roofs. Projecting from the nave, towards the road, is a lower and narrower west porch bay, with a south-west spire to its side. The spire stands square, with Romanesque type wheel window, and then becomes octagonal, with lancets. The nave bays are marked by buttresses.

Baptist Church, Hamstead Road, Handsworth. This was built in the Early English style by J.P. Osborne in 1883, and is Grade II listed. The facing materials are red sandstone with ashlar sandstone dressings. The front has a north-west tower, with pinnacled, angled buttresses and broached spire. The entrance has carved spandrel panels in two centred arches, with finialed and chequer-patterned gable over arcaded balustrade. The gable to the church is surmounted by a finial. On the south there is an apsidal-ended chapel, with gables to each face over coupled lights.

Baptist Chapel, Oxford Road, Moseley. J.P. Osborne submitted a design for the competition to design St Agnes's Church, Moseley, but did not win. However, the local Baptist congregation was so impressed with his scheme that a decision was taken to use it for the chapel the members were intending to build. The building has a clerestoried nave, buttressed narrow aisles, transepts, apsidal chancel, apsidal south-west baptistery and buttressed north-west tower, with pinnacles and spire. It is built in stone, is Grade II listed and Pevsner gives the date as 1888. J.A. Chatwin had submitted an application for a Baptist chapel in Oxford Road, Moseley, in 1882, but presumably it was not built.

Methodist Chapel, Lozells Street, Lozells was designed in 1893 by Crouch & Butler, and is Grade II listed. It is built in red brick, with stone dressings and has a slate roof. It is symmetrical in design, with a gabled centre and two bays each side, decreasing in height. The gable is flanked either side by brick turrets, crowned by a lantern. A large window below the gable is surmounted by a triplet of arches on a stone string course. The next block each side has a hipped roof and a single arched window. Beyond are the entrances, each with two arches separated by a column.

Methodist Chapel, Somerset Road, Handsworth. Crouch & Butler designed this chapel a year after Lozells Street. The main hall is at right angles to the road and is five bays long. The right bay projects forward to the pavement, as a porch, and has a gable.

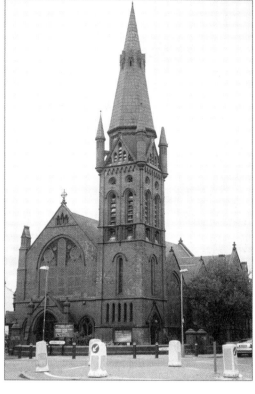

Above, left: Baptist church, Oxford Road, Moseley.

Above, right: Wesleyan Methodist church, King's Heath.

Left: Baptist church, Edward Road, Balsall Heath.

The main roof continues down over the other four bays to line up with the entrance front. The bays are separated by stone-capped buttresses and each contains a three-light window, with stone sill and head continued through. There are three dormer windows in the roof over the main hall, with swept heads. The right, buttressed end of the main hall has a five-light arched window. On the roof is an elaborate ventilating structure, with a weathervane. At the left there is a hall, with buttressed gable and a round-headed window. The main material is brick with stone dressings.

Wesleyan Methodist Church, School Road and Cambridge Road, King's Heath. William Hale was the architect of this 1896 church, which has a prominent tower in the south-west corner, with lancet windows, pinnacles and octagonal spire. The west front has a large arched window over the entrance porch, which is gabled between turrets. On the south side, there are twin gabled aisles and projecting gabled transept, with turrets.

Baptist Church, Edward Road, Balsall Heath is a Grade II listed church of 1899, designed by Ingall & Sons, with clerestoried nave, low aisles, transepts, and a Sunday school at rear. The principal material is red brick, with lavish buff terracotta ornament and dressings, in a style combining Romanesque and Perpendicular. The north entrance front has a broad, shaped gable, with flanking turrets, capped by terracotta, openwork cupolas. Above the porch is a pair of Romanesque windows and the gable has terracotta banding.

JEWISH

Synagogue, 26, 26A and 26B Blucher Street. This is another Grade II* listed building, designed by Yeoville Thomason and built in 1856. It is Italianate in style and built in red brick, with stone dressings. Centrally, there is a portico, with a rose window in the gable above. There are two-storey projecting wings at each side.

CHAPTER 11

THE JEWELLERY QUARTER & SURROUNDS

T he Jewellery Quarter is unique and precious, and is receiving a great amount of interest from English Heritage, and the number of buildings helping to arouse that interest is huge. Many of its industrial and commercial buildings are of interest. I shall start with a walk covering most of the buildings that I want to mention specifically, and you will pass many more of equal quality. After the walk, there will be a few buildings left that were a little out of our way, which I shall deal with separately. We start at the bottom of Constitution Hill and you will notice, in many cases, that I do not know the name of the architect, a matter of some regret to me.

1–7 Constitution Hill. This building, containing works and offices for H.B. Sale, was designed by Doubleday & Shaw in 1896 and is Grade II listed. It is sited at a

1–7 Constitution Hill and 394–6 Summer Lane.

prominent intersection and the architects took full advantage of this and designed an extravagantly detailed, four-storey, circular, terracotta tower, topped with an octagonal, arcaded turret and cupola. Another feature is its colour, provided by red brick and red terracotta. The main building is four storeys high, with shaped gables and different window treatments at each floor and from the tower. It is an asset to the area.

1–4 Hampton Street and 394–6 Summer Lane. This is a corner building of *c*. 1880, comprising shops and works, with housing and workshops above. The bowed corner and immediate returns are four storeys high and the main sides are three storeys high, plus attics. It is built in red brick, with stone, cut brick, ceramic brick and polychrome tile dressings and decoration. The corner shop had broad, articulating piers, while adjacent shops and works entrances have panelled pilasters, with elongated consoles and bracket cornices. Upper storeys have single and coupled windows and gables with roundels. There is a three-tiered, decorated oriel window at the corner, with a deep cornice breaking through the eaves. The building is Grade II listed.

25 Constitution Hill.

25 Constitution Hill is a tall, four-storey building on a prominent corner site, built in 1882–3 as a music warehouse; it is Grade II listed. It was occupied at the turn of the century, and probably earlier and later, by Joseph Riley, who sold pianos, a name that cropped up in Corporation Street. The external finishes are yellow and white brick, with ceramic brick pilasters. There is a deep stone entablature over the top floor and a yellow brick parapet.

As you walk along, notice the Hen and Chickens and the former Gothic public houses at 27 Constitution Hill and 1 Great Hampton Street, respectively.

22A Great Hampton Street and 61 Harford Street. One of the many branches of Lloyds Bank designed by J.A. Chatwin, this one in 1899, and Grade II listed. The building is two storeys high, plus an attic, and with a tall ground floor. The entrance is in the splayed corner and is surmounted by an oriel window and a polygonal cupola. There are three Dutch-type gables, all different. The first three windows to Great Hampton Street and four to Harford Street are the same, with a prominent keystone to the ground-floor windows and segmental-headed windows at first-floor. The end bay to each face fits in two floors within the general ground-floor height, with a canted bay window, with deep parapet, to Great Hampton Street and a segmental pediment over the window to Harford Street. The first-floor windows have

22A Great Hampton Street.

blind balustrades. In the gable to Great Hampton Street there is a two-light window, with a projecting balcony. The materials are stone and terracotta.

44 and 45 Great Hampton Street and 80–96 Hockley Street, known as the Pelican Works, was built in 1868, for Thomas Wilkinson & Sons and is Grade II listed. The building is two storeys high, with seven bays to Great Hampton Street and a four-bay return to the factory. The main facing material is red brick, with stucco dressings. The main entrance is from the central bay and there are three windows each side, with square heads at ground floor and segmental, stucco heads at first floor and panels under. There is a parapet, with openwork panels above the roof cornice, broken in the centre to accommodate a large, stone pelican. The return along Hockley Street, to the twenty-five-bay, three-storey factory building, is similar to the main front.

83 and 84 Great Hampton Street. Further down, and on the other side of the street, is this three-storey, Grade II listed building of *c.* 1880, built in red brick, with painted stone dress-ings. It is six bays wide, with the end bays slightly advanced, with gables over, and a stone coping between, incorporating three miniature gables. It is next door to a very prestigious building, namely

44 and 45 Great Hampton Street.

80–2 Great Hampton Street.

80–2 Great Hampton Street. This building was erected in 1872, the architect was Yeoville Thomason, and it is Grade II* listed. It was built as a jewellery works, in the Gothic style, and is three storeys high. The main facing material is red brick, with painted stone and engineering-brick dressings. It is capped with a bracketed cornice and parapet. Windows are in pointed arcades to the upper floors and at the ground floor are in pairs. The words 'Great Hampton Street Works' are in a band between ground and first floors. Crouch & Butler made applications for shopping in 1887 and two-storey shopping in 1891, both in Great Hampton Street, and for Green Cadbury, the owner of this important site.

I suggest you continue along Great Hampton Street and turn left into Vyse Street and visit the Museum of the Jewellery Quarter, at 75–9 Vyse Street. These were the premises of Smith & Pepper but, unfortunately for you, they were built too late for you to examine them in this context. After your visit continue along Vyse Street, turn left into Spencer Street and look at Plantagenet Buildings, on the right corner of Hockley Street. It is a three-storey building, of 1871, with an extremely narrow frontage to Hockley Street, but happily it widens out along Spencer Street. From here, proceed along Hockley Street turn left at Vyse Street, and further along you will see

9 Vyse Street. I have chosen this building, erected as a works and showroom, for its rather different appearance. It is noted as *c*. 1880, is three storeys high, four bays wide, symmetrical and built in brick and terracotta. At ground-floor level, doors at each side flank two central windows, with four centred, shallow arches in terracotta. The first-floor windows are arcaded, with ogee heads, and the second-floor windows are in a mullioned arcade. The roof is hipped, of slate, with finials flanking ridge tiles. The building is Grade II listed.

Continue to Warstone Lane, averting your eyes from the Jewellery Quarter Clock Tower as, unfortunately, it was built about three years after the Victorian era had ended; turn left along Warstone Lane, and on the opposite side of the road you will see two buildings, side by side. The first is

27 and 28 Warstone Lane. This building of *c.* 1860–70 is the elder of these two jewellery works and, as befits its age, the more restrained. It is three storeys high and has three windows at each level, grouped closely together in the centre. Unfortunately it was decided that an entrance was needed, and that is crammed in on the right side. The principal material is red brick, with gault-brick bands and stone dressings. The ground-floor windows are round-headed, the first-floor windows have segmental heads and the second-floor windows are cut into the frieze. The building is Grade II listed, as is its neighbour.

29 Warstone Lane. This building, of *c.* 1870, was determined to outdo its neighbour, not only by being more dressy, but by having an extra window in the width, achieved by using up more of the façade. The main facing material is red brick, with gault brick, tile and painted stone dressings. The piers between the ground-floor windows are wider than the ones above, so that they are not in line. The windows have arched heads, with emphasised keystones. Elaborate detailing, particularly at ground and first floors, at the arch springing, seems too heavy, but the five stone discs at second-floor level, between the first-floor arches, are a more attractive feature.

Both of the above buildings are an asset to the area, as is the next one you will see, after you have gone back along Warstone Lane to its junction with Tenby Street North and look at the building on the corner, now known as Aquinas House, but built for Manton & Mole, at

27–8 and 29
Warstone Lane.

63 Warstone Lane.

63 Warstone Lane. An application was made in 1882 for this building by H.L. Mole, and I assume he was involved as owner and not architect, but have not checked this. This is an interesting building, divided into two distinct sections along the Tenby Street North frontage. The first part, on the corner and extending along Warstone Lane, is the office section and is three storeys high, plus a sub-basement. The corner is splayed and projects slightly to form a tower from first-floor level upwards. It rises a little above eaves level and terminates with a pyramidal slate roof, topped with a weathervane. The office entrance is on the corner, with a head I find difficult to describe, with paired windows above, square-headed at first floor and round-headed to the second floor. Along Tenby Street North, this section has five windows, those at ground floor have shallow, segmental heads, at first-floor level they are round-headed, with carved infilling to the tympanum, and there are gables to the larger second and fourth windows at the second floor. All of these windows are of the sash type. The principal material to both sections is red brick.

The other section of the building contains the workshops and is in the window proportion 1.2.2.2.1, divided by flue stacks, projecting slightly up to the arch springing at first-floor level, where they are corbelled out. At ground floor the windows are shallow, with segmental heads, those at first floor are tall and round-headed. These windows are iron framed.

It is with some diffidence that I ask you to turn around and walk back along Warstone Lane and turn right into Vittoria Street, where there are many interesting buildings, including the School of Jewellery (mentioned in chapter 7 under Other Schools and Colleges). There are many I could name, but I will confine myself to one, a comparatively large one:

9 Vittoria Street. This was designed by Thomas F. Williams in 1879–80 and is on a corner site and was built as fifteen units. It is a long, three-storey building, of close-set bays to both frontages, with a rounded corner. The ground-floor doorways are round-headed and set in rusticated, painted stonework. Full-height brick piers separate the narrow window groups of three, with ground-floor entablature and first-floor sill band projecting forward with piers.

Go along Regent Place to

12 and 14 Regent Place. This Grade II listed building is a three-storey, Gothic-style manufactory, designed by A.H. Hamblin in 1883 and faced in red brick, with stone and moulded brick dressings. It has a symmetrical elevation, with two-bay gables flanking a central, three-bay gable, with paired and triple groupings of windows at second-floor level. The first-floor windows are in an arcade off a continuous sill band.

Return to Vittoria Street and walk down to the junction with Graham Street where, on the right corner, you will see

Victoria Works, Graham Street, which extends from Vittoria Street to Frederick Street, with its main frontage to Graham Street. The building was erected in 1839–40 for Joseph Gillott, the manufacturer of steel pen nibs. According to the introduction and guide to the area, produced by English Heritage, 100 million pen nibs were produced at the factory in 1853. The building is three storeys high, Grade II listed, built primarily of red brick, but with a stone plinth up to ground-floor window-sill level, a stone band below the first-floor windows and a deep band beneath the roof cornice, with a parapet above that to the central bay. There are three main bays to Graham Street, the central bay slightly advanced and five windows wide at the upper levels, with the central window wider and with a stone surround at first-floor level. The main entrance is in a stone surround, covering the width of three windows and up to first-floor window-sill level. The outer bays are three windows wide, with secondary entrances under the centre windows, which have a stone surround at first-floor level.

Victoria Works,
Graham Street.

Argent Centre, Legge Lane.

Walk along Graham Street to Frederick Street and, on the opposite corner you will see a jewel of the Jewellery Quarter:

The Argent Centre, Legge Lane and Frederick Street. I have attributed the design of this Grade II* listed building, of 1862–3, to J.G. Poland and, although I have no reason to doubt that this is correct, would not be in a position to substantiate it without further investigation. It is an Italianate building, of great presence, and the red-brick background gives a fine setting for its polychromatic patterning. Its frontage to Legge Lane, which I will refer to, is spoiled only, to me, by its incongruous entrance doorway and stone surround. The elevation is flanked by square, slightly advanced, four-storey towers, with three narrow, round-headed windows to the outer faces at third-floor level, and single windows at the lower levels. Between the towers there are seven bays of windows to the three-storey main section, six at ground floor plus the entrance, at the right. The building starts with a blue-brick plinth and there are one-course bands, sometimes joined together vertically at intervals, punctuating the red brickwork, up to the arch springing of the second-floor windows. The single windows, at ground floor, have round-headed arches, and above, piers rise off the first floor entablature, enfolding the coupled windows at first and second floors and the panels between, and finishing with round-headed arches. Above the cornice is a balustrade and high parapet. The building at one time housed a Turkish bath. It needs to be seen to appreciate its colour and patterning.

3, 4, and 5 Legge Lane. This Grade II listed building, of 1893, was designed by Essex, Nicol & Goodman for Cornelius Davenport, a manufacturer of pens and penholders. It is three storeys high and has seven close-set window bays. The main facing material is terracotta, with red brick to the lower part of the ground floor and rendered bands between storeys and in the parapet carried up to a tall, shaped gable. At the second floor there is a round-headed arcade, with rosettes in spandrels. There is a rich, terracotta frieze and ball finials above parapet kneelers and on the piers flanking the gable.

Now make your way down Newhall Hill, towards the Parade and on the way you will see

16 and 17 Newhall Hill, an interesting building of 1868–70, Grade II listed and designed by Yeoville Thomason. It is built in blue-brick, with red and grey brick and

16 and 17 Newhall Hill.

stone dressings. At ground-floor level there are blue-brick piers separating alternating openings of four narrow, round-headed and three wide, segmental-headed. The first-floor windows rise off a deep entablature, but with the revised rhythm of narrow (n) and wide (w) openings of 1n.1w.4n.1w.1n, caused by the replacement of the central segmental-headed opening with two round-headed openings. Between the arches there are discs and a string course over. A parapet with a blind balustrade pattern caps the building.

Having persuaded you to walk down Newhall Hill, I am going to ask you, when you reach the bottom, to turn left into George Street and walk along to Newhall Street, stopping on your way to observe

Newhall Works, George Street. This is a large, Grade II listed building, of about 1860–70, built in red brick. It is a symmetrical structure of twenty-seven bays, mainly three storey, but with a four-storey, central section. Nearly all openings are the same size, with segmental heads. There is a continuous, stucco, dentil course over the

Newhall Works,
George Street.

Birmingham Assay Office, Newhall Street.

second floor, and the third floor of the centre section has a range of small, arcaded windows, with a stucco cornice surmounted by the Royal Coat of Arms. The central three bays of each wing are advanced.

When you reach Newhall Street walk down to the

Birmingham Assay Office, Newhall Street. I feel this important building should be included, but it has had so many alterations and extensions, including at least two by Ewen Harper in 1891 and 1907, that I have decided to limit my description to a few words about the 1878 building, on the corner of Charlotte Street. The frontage to Newhall Street of this two-storey building (a third storey was added early in the twentieth century) is five bays wide and built in red brick, with stone dressings. The central bay is filled by the entrance, protected by a portico, with a balcony and open balustrade over. Above this there are two columns supporting the projecting roof cornice, which is crowned with a segmental pediment. The windows have segmental heads. It is an interesting place to go round. I have been twice on organised visits and assume that this would be the only way to find out what goes on inside.

That covers the last building of the walk, which I hope has not left you exhausted. There are a few others to mention, but I will leave you to see them in the order you wish.

105 Brearley Street, Newtown. This is the former Newey Goodman factory, buil in about 1840, and Grade II listed. It is a three-storey, three-bay wide, symmetrical building, with the centre bay slightly advanced and flanked by the outer bays, with three windows at the upper levels. At the ground-floor level a door with a segmental head takes the place of the outer window of each wing, and the second-floor windows are shallower. The main entrance is in the centre bay, and above the eaves entablature is, or was, 'J.G. Newey' and a coat of arms. The main facing material is brick, with a painted stone band above ground floor.

45 Great Charles Street and 12 New Market Street. This was designed by A.S. Dixon, the son of George Dixon, for the Birmingham Guild of Handicrafts, in 1895. It is a brick building, three storeys high, with gabled bays on the corner. The windows are casements, with semicircular heads at ground floor and segmental heads above. It is Grade II listed.

Birmingham Mint, Icknield Street. The Birmingham Mint has had many extensions over the years and has a long frontage to Icknield Street, but the part I am concerned with is of about 1860, long after the business was founded, and is a Grade II listed building. The front, to the street, is three storeys high, built in red brick and is symmetrical in a bay arrangement of 2.5.1.5.2. The centre bay is wider, with a triangular pediment, and projects forward, as do the outer bays with their hipped roofs. In the centre bay there is a large, round-headed archway, with a keystone angled out, to support a two-storey stone tripartite bow window.

Pumping Station, Waterworks Road, Edgbaston. Martin & Chamberlain designed pumping stations at Longbridge and Selly Oak, in addition to this one, erected in about 1870 and Grade II listed. The complex includes several buildings, the main ones being the pump house and the stack, and I shall confine myself to those. The buildings are built in bricks of many colours, mainly red. The pump house is a tall, gabled building, with tall, lancet windows at the lower levels and smaller ones over. There is a roundel in the gable.

It has been suggested that the chimney stack and the adjoining **Perrott's Folly** were the inspirational source for the Towers of Gondor, in Tolkien's *Lord of the Rings*. It is an impressive structure, square in plan and divided vertically into stages. The first has broad, lancet windows, the second has two light windows, the third has single lancets and the fourth has coupled windows. I have not mentioned the various decorative bands. Above all this there is a balcony with iron railings, an octagonal turret, with lancets in the sides, and then a spire, truncated soon after birth.

78 and 79 Broad Street. This building was erected in 1898 by Bateman & Bateman, for Barclays Bank, on the corner of Sheepcote Street and is Grade II listed. It is three storeys high, with an attic, and six windows long to Broad Street and with two similar windows to Sheepcote Street, separated by a wide chimney stack. The ground floor is

Birmingham Mint,
Icknield Street.

266 and 266X Broad Street.

faced in banded stonework, with an almost triangular projection on the corner, containing the main entrance, with a balcony and balustrade over. From first-floor level the main facing material is red brick, with alternating stone quoins at the corners and to the chimney stack and with stone dressings to the windows. The tall first-floor windows have shallow balconies, with metal railings, and the second-floor windows are shallow, to compensate. Above the bracketed cornice there are gabled dormers. The bank has become a restaurant, the Left Bank, but you are lucky if you can get a table that enables you to see the river.

266 and 266X Broad Street and 2 Gas Street. An application was made by Martin & Chamberlain, in 1887, for 'Shop, Offices and Warehouses', on behalf of Joseph Sturge, and this was followed, in 1896, by an application for extensions. This is a Grade II listed building, mainly two storeys plus attic, but part is three storeys. The principal facing material is red brick, with some stone dressings. There are two large and three small gables, the latter having coupled arched windows at first floor, with an octofoil set in stone over, and cut brick above that. The building was Merchant Stores public house, but at the time of writing is Scruffy Duffys.

266A–271 Broad Street. I became aware of this building through its next-door neighbour. It is a three-storey, *c.* 1880, Venetian Gothic-style building, Grade II listed, having a window pattern, at first and second-floor levels, of 3.2.2.2.2.3. These windows, rising off string courses, have arched heads with blind tympana. It has a patterned and bracketed parapet. It was, and probably still is, the Walkabout Inn.

I shall leave you here to make your own way home, or wait for the evening's entertainment to commence.

CHAPTER 12

PUBLIC HOUSES

Before I started on this chapter I thought it would be one of the easiest, and that it would be a case of deciding which buildings to leave out, whereas the difficulty has been in finding any to include. The problem has been twofold: the general standard of buildings is not high and some of the best have disappeared; and there is a great deal of similarity between buildings, for, particularly in the 1890s when many public houses were built or rebuilt, a formula was used for both layout and appearance, which was emphasised by the use of the same few architects for most of the buildings. I have made a small selection, including some which are representative of many others.

The Trocadero and Albert Chambers, 17 and 18 Temple Street. I may not be completely correct in including this mid-nineteenth-century Grade II listed building in this category, for it was not built as a public house and this use came later in the century, when the building was altered and the attractive tilework – mainly yellow – pilasters and frieze, incorporating the names, were added. The building, attributed to Charles Edge, is three storeys high and three bays wide at first- and second-floor levels.

The outer bays are slightly advanced, with boldly cut quoins. They have a single sash window at each level and the centre bay has two windows at each level. There are entablatures at first-floor window-sill level and second-floor level, and the frieze above the second-floor windows of the centre bay has a block pattern design.

The Gothic, 1, 1A and 1B Great Hampton Street. This building was erected as a public house but no longer fulfills that purpose. I have seen different dates given for the erection of this three-storey, Grade II listed building with attic, but think late 1870s is reasonable. The main features of the building are at the splayed corner, starting with an oriel window at first-floor level, over the

The Trocadero, 17 and 18 Temple Street.

Above: Hen & Chickens, 27–9 Constitution Hill.

Left: The Gothic, 1, 1A and 1B Great Hampton Street.

entrance and terminating with a gabled dormer and an octagonal turret, with a short slate spire. All of the windows are arched, with different detailing at each level.

Hen & Chickens, 27–9 Constitution Hill. An elegant, Grade II listed, public house of *c.* 1880, on the corner of Henrietta Street, with the popular splayed entrance feature. The building is three storeys high, with an entablature at first-floor level, and is capped with a bracketed cornice and parapet. The main feature of the building is the treatment of the first and second floors. At the upper floors it has four equal bays to Henrietta Street and three bays to Constitution Hill, with the outer one, in this case, being wider. The bays are separated by banded piers, rising from a plinth on the first-floor entablature and terminating, with a capping, at the arch springing to the second-floor windows. The normal-width bays have a segmental-headed window at first-floor level and two round-headed windows at the second floor. The wider bay has two narrower, segmental-headed windows at first floor and three round-headed windows, of the same width as the others, at second-floor level. The corner has single round-headed windows at each level. There is a decorated panel between the upper and lower windows.

New Inns, Holyhead Road, Handsworth. This is a Grade II listed building of 1881, with an extension of 1901 on the right side. It is built in red brick and sandstone and is a symmetrical composition, with two-storey, gabled wings and a three-storey central block, with paired gables.

Yorkshire Grey, 381 Dudley Road and 1 Winson Street. I have chosen this building for two reasons: firstly, it is simple, attractive and different from the others, and secondly, it was designed by Henry Naden, the architect of the Woodman, on Easy

Row. Despite taking second place in the building's address, the main length of the building is to Winson Street. There is a splayed corner at ground floor, to accommodate the entrance door, but this changes to a curve at the frieze over the ground-floor windows. The building is three storeys high and has a hipped roof to the Dudley Road frontage and the first half of the Winson Street frontage, and then drops to two storeys, with a parapet. The windows at the upper levels are sash type and have segmental heads at the second floor. The ground-floor windows are three lights wide, with a transom, and have slim pilasters between. The finish to the upper floors is stucco.

Red Lion, 53–5 Church Street. This was the rebuilding for Alfred Homer, in 1898, of an old public house of the same name by A.H. Hamblin, and it stands on the corner of Cornwall Street. The name was changed about forty years ago; it is known now as the Old Royal and is Grade II listed. From a comparatively restrained ground floor, with round-headed openings and splayed corner, the building explodes into life at the first and second floors, starting with an oriel window at the corner, with various bands of decoration over the upper window, terminating in a conical roof. The next two bays along Church Street and one along Cornwall Street are constrained by piers terminating in pinnacles. These bays have canted bay windows at first floor, with a balustrade over, and the floor above has two round-headed windows, with a matching pier between and all finished with a decorated shaped gable. Beyond, on Church Street, there is a single window bay, with piers and pinnacles as before and a balustrade between, and this is more than matched on Cornwall Street, with three bays, except that the last two bays each have two windows at each level. The facing materials are bricks and terracotta.

The Britannia Inn, 287 Lichfield Road, Aston. To some extent this building is like the emperor with no clothes, for the buildings which covered its less attractive features

Red Lion (the Old Royal), 53–5 Church Street.

Red Lion, 105 Station Road, Erdington.

have disappeared and left it naked, to be seen by the train passengers on the Lichfield line. It is a three-storey building, plus an attic, is Grade II listed, designed by Wood & Kendrick, and was built in the period 1898–1900. The main part of the frontage is projected forward, with canted sides going back to recessed single doorways at each end, protected by balustrades over, following the line of the projection and supported by scrolled brackets at the ends. Above the ground floor the projecting section is in the window proportion of 1.2.1, with a triangular pediment over the two-light window at first-floor level. The second-floor windows are semicircular-headed, and above there is a central feature over the double window, containing a three-light window and surmounted by a figure of Britannia. There is an open-fronted balustrade to the remainder at roof level.

There are, or were, probably more public houses of importance along Lichfield Road than anywhere else in the city.

Red Lion, 105 Station Road and Short Heath Road, Erdington. Having mentioned one public house by Wood & Kendrick, what could be easier than to mention another? This is a large building, erected in 1899, with long frontages to both roads, built principally of brick, but with stone banding to the first floor. There is a square clock tower on the corner, with the obligatory entrance door under a pedimented head. There are four bays to the two-storey Station Road frontage, with large segmental-headed windows at first floor, in the second and fourth bays, surmounted by semicircular gables, flanked by finials topping the separating piers. A bow-fronted oriel window is crammed into the third bay, The first bay along Short Heath Road matches the other first bay, and then there are two bays, with an attic, and open-pedimented heads to the two windows.

The Fighting Cocks, St Mary's Row and King Edward Road, Moseley. This is, possibly, the best known of all the buildings designed by Newton & Cheatle outside

The Fighting Cocks,
St Mary's Row, Moseley.
Inset: This barometer is
set into the stonework at
the side of the main
doorway.

the city centre. It is Grade II listed, was built in 1899, and is faced in brick and stone. It is two storeys high along King Edward Road and three storeys high to St Mary's Row. There is an elegant, octagonal, stone clock tower on the corner, crowned by a bell-shaped cupola. There is no great rhythm to the King Edward Road elevation, but there are two shallow canted bay windows at first-floor level, of different widths. The frontage to St Mary's Row is more regular, with four bays, having shaped gables separated by narrow bays, with the windows and stone panels slightly recessed. The project was for a public house and two shops and, I think, the public house covered only two of the gabled bays, which have a canted bay window at first-floor level and a parapet over, rising to the second-floor window sill. I believe it is not too difficult to recognise this as a public house, but, most definitely, a public house of the superior sort.

The Dog and Partridge, 210 Moseley Street. It is time to include a public house by James & Lister Lea, the most prolific of all pub architects, and I have chosen this one, built on the corner of Birchall Street in 1900, as typical of the practice's work of the period. I saw it regularly at one time, as I designed a building close by, and the work included alterations to existing buildings that wrapped themselves around the Dog and Partridge. It is likely that it was designed by Mr Roberts, whom I knew during the Second World War. The wide ground-floor windows are segmental and the narrower openings are round-headed. There is an oriel rising through two floors and crowned with a cupola, above the bevelled corner. There are two gables to Moseley Street and one to Burchall Street, above deep segmental-headed windows at second-floor level, with decorative panels reaching down from the sills to connect to the semicircular features above the first-floor windows. The finishes are brick and terracotta.

Church Tavern, 1 Waterworks Street and Lichfield Road, Aston. A two-storey high building, erected in 1900–1, with a splayed corner, and three bays in each direction, and finished in brick and terracotta. At ground floor the two bays closest to the corner have wide segmental-headed windows and the doorways have triangular pediments over. At the corner there is a polygonal oriel window with a slate spire, and the centre bays have canted bay windows at first floor. The building is Grade II listed and was designed by C.H. Collett.

The Barton's Arms, 144 High Street, Aston.
(Birmingham Central Library)

The Barton's Arms, 144 High Street and Potter's Lane, Aston. This Grade II* listed building of 1900–1 is looked upon as James & Lister Lea's public house masterpiece, and few would argue about this. The two streets converge from a northerly direction in an arrow-like fashion, but with a substantial part of the tip missing, leaving quite a wide south front, which is prominent from the lower part of High Street. This elevation has a wide, two-storey canted bay, with parapet, below two round-headed windows and a shaped gable, as a central feature. At the sides of this eleva-

tion there are angled door openings with triangular pediments some way above. The main, west front, to High Street, is divided into six bays, with the fourth from the left different from the others. This bay is narrower, has a balcony at first floor and is surmounted by a clock tower, rising above eaves level and with the name below the clocks. The other five bays have wide, segmental-headed windows in the stone-faced ground-floor front. The upper floors are in brick, with shallow, canted bay windows at first-floor level, tripartite windows at second floor, with sharply swept pediments over, and crowned with Dutch gables. A very interesting building.

Selly Park Hotel, 592 Pershore Road, Selly Oak. This building was erected in 1901 and is now known as the Selly Park Tavern. It is a symmetrical building, with the main, central section three storeys high and flanked by recessed, narrow, two-storey wings, with secondary entrances and capped with shaped parapets. The central section is three bays wide, with the main entrance in the centre bay, which terminates in a gable. Each outer bay has a two-storey, canted bay window and parapet, with a blank wall over, terminating in a shaped parapet leading to gable ends. The principal material is brick, with some banding.

As with other building types, I have confined my descriptions to the exteriors, but the interiors of many public houses are often imposing and, in some cases, more renowned than the exteriors that enclose them. An advantage of public houses, unlike many other buildings, is that the interiors are open to the public during normal opening hours – at a reasonable cost.

CHAPTER 13

A MISCELLANY

I reserved this section for buildings that I thought would not fit happily into the other categories and believed there would be a large number, but I was wrong. The number has been reduced, also, by deciding that buildings selected in this category would be better somewhere else. You may think that, of the few remaining buildings, some are unnecessarily included, but I felt I had gone far enough and daren't reduce the numbers more, so please bear with me, while I start with a flourish:

Curzon Street Station, Curzon Street, was the original terminus of the London–Birmingham railway and, although it didn't retain the position for long because the line was extended to New Street in the early 1850s, the building has survived, unlike the Euston Arch at the London end of the line. Originally there were side wings, through which the passengers passed, but they disappeared long ago, as did the adjoining hotel building. The three-storey, three-bays wide and three-bays deep Grade I listed building was erected in 1838 and the architect was Philip Hardwick. The main feature is the giant portico, supported on four Ionic columns, built off block bases, with a gap in the centre leading to the round-headed entrance, which is surmounted by a coat of arms. The outer first-floor windows, under the portico, have blind balconies but after these it is hard to find any decorative features to describe. The virtues of the building are found in the sense of strength, simplicity and proportion, producing a great building. It is very easily seen from the railway when travelling on the east side to and from New Street station, and Millennium Point is situated a short distance away. A new use is being sought for the building of the monument.

Curzon Street station.

Hall and Institute, Jenkins Street and Camelot Way is a tall, three-storey brick building of no great elegance, which I came across when looking for Board schools and it stands out prominently in an area where many buildings have been demolished. I discovered that it had been designed by Ewen Harper in 1893, I believe as a Methodist centre, had had many uses, and is now occupied by the Birmingham Community Association. The gabled entrance front faces Camelot Way and is three bays wide and dominated by the wide centre bay, flanked by polygonal buttresses, passing through the gable and finishing with cupola-like cappings. The wide, segmental-headed entrance is set in a surround, with a triangular pediment over the middle part. A wide window feature rises through the two floors above, finishing with a segmental head. In each outer bay there is a narrower, shorter window feature. The Jenkins Street frontage has five equal bays, then a secondary entrance bay, followed by a wider, gabled bay that appears to be part of the building, but a little unwanted.

Moseley and Balsall Heath Institute, Moseley Road.

Moseley and Balsall Heath Institute, Moseley Road. This is a building of unknown vintage to me, but I would think about 1870s. William Hale designed an extension for it in 1896 and it is likely that he was the architect for the original busy, Gothic-style building. It is two storeys high, with a sub-basement, and three bays wide, with flanking walls at each side. Each bay has a decorated gable, with three-light lancet windows, and is flanked by finials and at the apex. The centre bay contains the entrance, approached up steps, with an arched head, under a slightly projecting gable and with roundels on either side. At each side there is a triple window, with infilled arched heads. The roof is steep, with gable ends.

Friends' Hall and Institute, Moseley Road, Balsall Heath.

Friends' Hall and Institute, Moseley Road. I found the rear of this Quaker building while searching for somewhere else, went round to Moseley Road to see what the front looked like and was pleasantly surprised. That was a few years ago. The architect for this 1897 building was Ewen Harper. It is two storeys high, with three main bays and narrow flanking sections. The ground floor is stone faced, with a stone balustrade over, up to first-floor window-sill level. The centre bay has a projecting porch, forming a generous balcony to the window above, and containing the round-headed entrance opening. The first floor has three tall, shallow canted bay windows, with elaborate heads, leading up to three shaped gables, having

Carnegie Infant Welfare Institute,
Hunter's Road, Lozells.

stone banding and dressings. The side wall to the building is blank, as a contrast to its frontage. The principal material, except for the ground-floor front, is red brick.

Carnegie Infant Welfare Institute, Hunter's Road, Lozells. I have no record of the date this building by J.L. Ball was erected, although I believe it is late nineteenth century. It is a three-storey brick building, its site sloping along the front. There is a projecting bay at the right, containing the round-headed entrance and a window, with iron balustrade over. Then there are ten bays, having round-headed, arched openings at ground floor. At first and second floors, in slightly recessed panels between piers, are windows with balustrades. Just below the first-floor string course there are five discs between the openings in the rhythm of 1.2.2.2.2.1. At the top of the building is a triangular brick pattern. A lower, narrower bay, at the left, completes the building.

I will finish with what was a popular feature in the parks in late Victorian times, and will deal with three examples, all of which are Grade II listed:

Handsworth Park, Hinstock Road has a late Victorian bandstand, octagonal in plan, having a brick base, iron Corinthian columns, elaborate ironwork, domed roof, cupola and weathervane. As a bonus, there is also an umbrello, Grade II listed, presented by Austin B. Lines in 1888.

Cannon Hill Park, Pershore Road, Edgbaston. This is another octagonal bandstand, *c.* 1880–90, with a brick platform, cast-iron columns, brackets, decorative pierced work, a swept conical-shaped roof, lantern cupola with scrolled, pierced panels, topped with a small ogee spirelet, ball finial and weathervane.

Botanical Gardens, Westbourne Road, Edgbaston. This bandstand is an elongated octagon in plan, with a stepped plinth of blue and buff bricks and a platform of red and blue bricks. Twisted Corinthian columns carry four centred arches with openwork spandrels. Three of the sides have glazed screens. The hipped roofs have patterned slates with two iron finials. Other parts to see include the West Terrace of 1865 and the Palm House of 1871, both Grade II listed, but I conclude here, at one of the jewels in Birmingham's crown.

BIBLIOGRAPHY

Bartlam, Norman, *Ladywood in Old Photographs*, Sutton, 1999

——, *Ladywood Revisited*, Sutton, 2001

Baxter, Marian, *Sutton Coldfield*, Alan Sutton, 1994

Baxter, Marian, and Drake, Peter, *Erdington*, Chalford, 1995

——, *Moseley, Balsall Heath and Highgate*, Chalford 1996

Bealby-Wright, Edmund, *Sketchbook Guide to the City of Birmingham*, Sketchbook Guides, 1993

Birmingham City Council, *Developing Birmingham 1889–1989*, Birmingham City Council, 1989

Bunce, J.T., *History of the Corporation of Birmingham, Volume 2, 1852–1884*, Cornish Brothers, 1885

Chatwin, Philip B., *Life Story of J.A. Chatwin*, 1952, Oxford University Press

Chinn, Carl, *Homes for People*, Brewin, 1999

Crawford, Alan (ed.), *By Hammer and Hand*, Birmingham Museums and Art Gallery, 1984

Crawford, Alan and Thorne, Robert, *Birmingham Pubs 1880–1939*, University of Birmingham, 1975

Davey, Peter, *Arts and Crafts Architecture*, Architectural Press, 1980

Dent, Robert K., *Old and New Birmingham, Volume 3*, Pub. weekly 1878–80, Houghton & Hammond, Birmingham. Repub. 1973 E.P. Publishing.

——, *Making of Birmingham*, J.L. Allday, 1894

Dixon, Roger and Muthesus, Stefan, *Victorian Architecture*, Thames & Hudson, 1978

Douglas, Alton, *Birmingham Remembered*, Birmingham Post & Mail, 1988

Drake, Peter, *Handsworth, Hockley and Handsworth Wood*, Tempus, 1998

——, *Winson Green and Brookfield*, Tempus, 2003

English Heritage, *The Birmingham Jewellery Quarter – an Introduction and Guide*, 2000

Green, Margaret D., *King's Heath*, Tempus, 1998

——, *Small Heath and Sparkbrook*, Tempus, 2002

Hampson, Martin, *Edgbaston*, Tempus, 1999

——, *Harborne, the Second Selection*, Tempus, 2002

Harding, Mary, *Birmingham Hospitals*, Reflections of a Bygone Age, 1999

Harrison, Michael, *Bournville*, Phillimore, 1999

Hickman, Douglas, *Shell Guide – Warwickshire*, Faber & Faber, 1979

Little, Bryan, *Birmingham Buildings*, David & Charles, 1971

Maxam, Andrew, *Time, Please*, Crown Cards, 2002

McKenna, Joseph, *Birmingham as it was – The City 1857–1914*, Birmingham Public Libraries, 1979

Pevsner, Nikolaus and Wedgwood, Alexandra, *The Buildings of England – Warwickshire*, Penguin, 1966

Reilly, John W., *Policing Birmingham*, West Midlands Police, 1989

Richardson, Amy, *Looking at Birmingham*, Brewin, 1994

Shackley, Barbara, *Three City Trails*, Victorian Society – Birmingham Group, 1998

Skipp, Victor, *The Making of Victorian Birmingham*, Victor Skipp, 1983

Turner, Keith, *Central Birmingham 1870–1920*, Alan Sutton, 1994

Twist, Maria, *Aston and Perry Barr*, Tempus, 1999

——, *Saltley, Duddeston and Nechells*, Tempus, 2001

Upton, Chris, *A History of Birmingham*, Phillimore, 1993

Vince, C.A., *History of the Corporation of Birmingham, Volume 3, 1885–1899*, Cornish Brothers, 1902

Whybrow, John, *How does your Birmingham grow?*, John Whybrow, 1972

——, *How Birmingham became a Great City*, John Whybrow, 1976

I have also consulted:

List of Buildings of Special Architectural or Historic Interest, two volumes

School Board Minutes of Birmingham, Aston, King's Norton, Yardley and Harborne

Registers of Building Plans of Birmingham, Aston and King's Norton

A History of the County of Warwick, Volume VII, Birmingham

Kelly's Directories